200 jams & preserves

Quince paste

Apple, apricot, & elderflower butter

St. Clement's curd

hamlyn | all color cookbook

200 jams & preserves

Sara Lewis

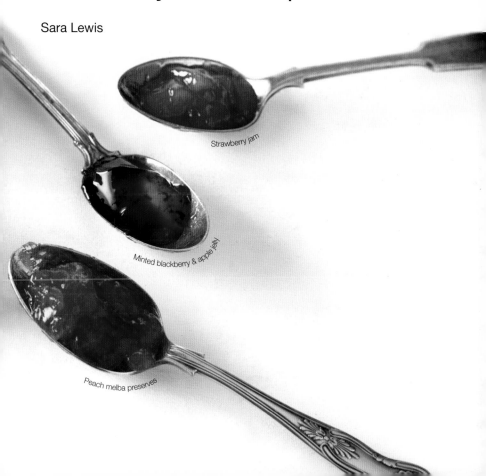

Strawberry jam

Minted blackberry & apple jelly

Peach melba preserves

An Hachette UK Company
www.hachette.co.uk

First published in Great Britain in 2012 by Hamlyn, a division
of Octopus Publishing Group Ltd, Endeavour House,
189 Shaftesbury Avenue, London WC2H 8JY
www.octopusbooks.co.uk
www.octopusbooksusa.com

Distributed in the US by Hachette Book Group USA
237 Park Avenue, New York NY 10017 USA

Distributed in Canada by Canadian Manda Group
165 Dufferin Street, Toronto, Ontario, Canada M6K 3H6

ISBN: 978-0-600-62510-0

Printed and bound in China

1 2 3 4 5 6 7 8 9 10

Standard level spoon measurements are used in all recipes.

Large eggs should be used unless otherwise stated. Freshly
ground black pepper should be used unless otherwise
stated. Because brands vary, please check the pectin
package directions to confirm the correct quantities to use.

Every effort has been made to ensure that all the information
in this book is accurate. However, due to differing conditions,
tools, and individual skills, the publisher cannot be
responsible for any injuries, losses, and other damages that
may result from the use of the information in this book.

This book includes dishes made with nuts and nut
derivatives. It is advisable for those with known allergic
reactions to nuts and nut derivatives or those who may be
potentially vulnerable to these allergies, such as pregnant and
nursing mothers, people with weakened immune systems, the
elderly, babies, and children, to avoid dishes made with these.

The U.S. Food and Drug Administration advises that eggs
should not be consumed raw. This book contains some
dishes made with raw or lightly cooked eggs. It is prudent
for more vulnerable people, such as pregnant and nursing
mothers, people with weakened immune systems, the
elderly, babies, and young children to avoid uncooked or
lightly cooked dishes made with eggs.

contents

introduction   6

jams, preserves, & conserves   18

fruit butters, curds, & pastes   66

jellies   92

marmalades   114

chutneys   134

relishes   166

pickles   184

festive fruit preserves   208

index   234

acknowledgments   240

introduction

introduction

In both the United States and Great Britain, making homemade preserves is going through a revival as the trend for using local produce grows. Nothing is more rewarding than picking your own fruit and gathering enough strawberries to can a few pints of jam, or growing your own fruit and vegetables to make chutneys and pickles. These recipes were originated for the British market, but have been adapted to include the canning process advised by the United States Food and Drug Administration. Unless stored in the refrigerator and used within a few weeks, preserves need to be processed in a water bath canner or pressure canner for safe, long-term storage.

If you are new to making preserves and the canning process, read through the introduction before you begin. Preserves are not difficult to make, but it is important to maintain the balance of fruit to sugar when making jams, jellies, or marmalade, or sugar to vinegar when making chutney. A chutney or a fruit curd is perhaps the best place to start; there are no tests for setting required—just keep cooking and stirring until thick. Once canned, they make great gifts, especially if packaged with ribbons or raffia and decorative labels. Preparing jams, jellies, and marmalades requires a little more attention, but the finished results are worth the care. Over the next few pages, you will find all the information you need.

Who's who

Here's a brief explanation of some of the terms used for various types of preserved produce.

Chutneys: These are sweet and sour and made with vinegar, sugar, spices, and chopped fresh fruits, dried fruits, usually with a base of chopped onions plus tomatoes or cooking apples. All the ingredients are added to the pot at once, then cooked "low and slow" until thick. Serve with cheese, cold meats, or sausages, or add to sandwiches.

Conserves: Similar to a jam but with a slightly softer set, these have a high proportion of large or whole pieces of fruit. Boil with sugar until setting point is reached. Serve spread on bread or toast, or spoon over ice cream.

Jams: Most often made with crushed or diced fruits. Boil with sugar until setting point is reached. Firmer than a conserve but not as set as a jelly.

Jellies: A crystal-clear preserve, best made with fruits that have seeds or that are time-consuming to prepare, because the fruit just needs to be chopped with no need to peel or core. Cook gently just covered with water until soft, then strain through a jelly bag. Add 2½ cups of sugar for every 2½ cups of strained liquid. Boil until setting point is reached. Serve in the same way as a jam. Savory jellies can be made with a mixture of water and vinegar, boiled with sugar, and flavored with herbs, spices, or peppercorns. Delicious served with roasted meat, game, broiled fish, or cold ham.

Fruit butters: A kind of jam made with poached fruit that is pureed and strained. For every 1 pound of puree, add between 1¼ cups and 2 cups of sugar, then cook gently until reduced almost by half and the mixture is thick and glossy. Somewhat like a chutney, these don't need to be boiled to reach setting point.

Fruit pastes: Quince paste, or membrillo, is perhaps the most popular. Also referred to as a fruit cheese, the concoction is made with a fruit puree but with a higher ratio of sugar at 2 cups to 2½ cups of sugar to every 1 pound of puree. Like fruit butter, the mixture is cooked gently until reduced and very thick. However, because there is more sugar, it sets firmly and is best spooned into oiled, wide-neck jars. Serve sliced alongside cheese.

Fruit curds: The most popular is perhaps lemon curd, where fruit juice and grated fruit rind is mixed with sugar, butter, and beaten eggs and cooked in a bain-marie or a bowl set over a saucepan of gently simmering water until thick. Fruit curds can also be made with pureed fruits, but this method is most suited to sharper, more acidic fruits, such as apples, gooseberries, or berries mixed with a citrus fruit. Because they contain eggs and butter, fruit curds must be stored in the refrigerator and consumed within a few weeks.

Marmalades: Traditionally made with whole Seville oranges that are cooked until soft, then finely cut into strips and boiled with sugar until setting point is reached. Because the availability of Seville oranges is so short, generally only between December and February, an alternative is to use a variety of oranges and mix with lemons and limes.

Mincemeat: A Christmas preserve made with boozy soaked dried fruits, grated apple, sugar, and spices and served in pastry shells.

Pickles: These can be made with vegetables, first soaked in a dry salt mix or brine to draw out the juices, then rinsed and packed while raw or blanched for a few minutes with flavored vinegar or a thickened spiced vinegar. Whole apricots or plums or halved peaches can also be pickled in a sweetened vinegar mix. Serve with salads, cold meats, cheese, or smoked fish.

Relishes: These can be cooked or uncooked and tend to be hotter and more intense than chutneys. Serve with curries, cold meats, or barbecued foods. Uncooked relishes must be stored in the refrigerator and served within a day or two of making.

equipment

Must-haves

Canner and accessories: A boiling-water canner is basically a large enamel pot that comes with a lid and a rack with handles; the rack prevents the jars from sitting directly on the bottom of the canner, so that water can circulate underneath them. If you have an electric stove or range, the canner must have a flat bottom (not all do) and it should be no more than 4 inches wider than the heating element. You can use a large, stainless steel stockpot as long as it is 3 inches deeper than the canning jars when set on a rack; you can use a circular cake cooling rack, or you can tie together several screw bands from canning jars. If you use a stockpot, you will also need a jar lifter, which looks like a pair of tongs and are designed to lift and lower jars into the water. For low-acid foods that won't have acidity added, you must use a pressure canner, which has either a weighted gauge or dial gauge for determining pressure.

Skimming spoon: A large, flat spoon with small perforations used to remove scum easily from the surface of the boiling jam.

Candy thermometer: This thermometer is the most accurate way to check the doneness of jams and jellies prepared without pectin.

Canning funnel: This has a top the size of a small plate or saucer with a wide-neck spout that is about 1½ inches long, so that it sits easily over a jar. Invaluable for ladling or pouring jam into jars to minimize spills.

Jelly bag: This cone-shaped bag can be made with cheesecloth, muslin, or fine nylon

mesh. It has strings or long loops at the top so that the bag can be suspended from a frame over a large bowl (make sure to rinse the bowl and bag with boiling water before use). It is great for making jellies. Spoon in the cooked fruit and water and let drip for 3–4 hours, or overnight. Resist the urge to squeeze the bag or the juice will be cloudy. The closer the mesh or weave of the fabric, the clearer the juice will be. If you are new to canning, or not sure how often you will use a jelly bag, improvise with a double-thickness layer of cheesecloth that has been soaked in boiling water, then draped into a large nylon strainer set over a bowl. After use, empty the jelly bag and wash well in hot water, but don't use detergent. Dry thoroughly before storing in a plastic bag.

Cheesecloth and string: You can buy cheesecloth at grocery stores and retail stores that sell kitchen supplies. Cut off as much as you need and soak in boiling water for 5 minutes to sterilize before use. Drain and let stand until cool enough to handle. Use to wrap whole spices, or citrus fruit seeds and pith, and tie with string before adding to the pot. Squeeze well at the end of cooking and discard the contents; wash and recycle the cheesecloth, depending on size.

Scales: Accuracy is important to make sure you have a good gelling set, so invest in kitchen scales, available from stores that sell cookware and kitchen gadgets, for weighing large amounts of fruit and vegetables.

Items that you are sure to have

Pots and pans: You'll need medium and large, heavy, stainless steel saucepans for cooking the ingredients before canning them. Good-quality ones will provide the best results.

Wooden spoons, ladle, spatula: Choose a wooden spoon with a long handle. Use only a plastic or rubber spatula, not a metallic one.

Measuring cups and spoons: Use standard kitchen measuring cups and spoons for both liquids and dry ingredients; for dry ingredients, the measurements should be level.

Lemon squeezer: For squeezing juice from citrus fruits.

Fine strainer: Choose a nylon or stainless-steel strainer so there is no chance that the fruit or vinegar will react with the strainer.

Vegetable peeler: To pare the fruit rind thinly with the minimum amount of pith.

Cutting board and knives: Choose a large wooden cutting board. You'll also need a small vegetable knife for removing pith and membrane from oranges or coring apples, plus a large knife for finely shredding pared citrus rind or dicing fruit and vegetables.

The ingredients

Many fruits can be used in jams, jellies, and preserves. Fruits differ in the amount of pectin they contain (see right), and slightly underripe fruit has more pectin than ripe fruit. Pectin is the gel-like substance essential to set jam and is found in varying amounts in the seeds, cores, and skins of fruits. When fruits are crushed and warmed, the pectin is released and mixes with the natural fruit acids to produce a gelatin-like set. Fruits with lower amounts of pectin can be mixed with fruits with higher levels. Choose fruit that is ripe (not overripe) and fresh for the maximum flavor and pectin, and wash before use.

Adding lemon juice or commercially prepared citric acid, available from pharmacies and health food stores, can help the fruit set. Low-acid fruits might also need pectin to be added. Commerical powdered and liquid pectin (made from natural ingredients) are available at supermarkets. Powdered pectin must be added before the sugar, but liquid pectin after the mixture is boiled. Confirm the details in the

----

making jams, jellies, & marmalades

Step-by-step guide

1 If you are not adding pectin or lemon juice, cook the fruit with a little water over gentle heat until just softened. Cook covered or uncovered as specified in the recipe. Stir often to release the pectin in the fruit and to prevent it from sticking. The pan should be no more than halfway full.

If using powdered pectin, add it to the crushed fruit with any flavorings and mix until the pectin has completely dissolved.

2 If not using pectin, add the sugar and stir gently, still over low heat, with a wooden spoon until the sugar completely dissolves.

PECTIN LEVELS

HIGH	cooking apples or sour, green eating-out-of-hand apples, crab apples, cranberries, black, red, and white currants, damsons, underripe gooseberries, grapefruit, grapes, japonicas, lemons, limes, loganberries, oranges, firm plums, quinces, rowanberries.
MEDIUM	eating-out-of-hand apples, fresh apricots, early blackberries, morello or may duke cherries, greengages, loganberries, mulberries, ripe plums, underripe raspberries.
LOW	sweet cherries, elderberries, medlars, melons, peaches, pears, pineapples, rhubarb, strawberries.

3 Increase the heat and bring to a boil (adding liquid pectin at this stage, if using) until setting point is reached, stirring occasionally.

Alternatively, if using powdered pectin, bring to a boil before adding the sugar, return to a boil, then boil for 1 minute.

4 Skim the jam, if needed, with a skimming spoon, or stir in 1–2 tablespoons butter to disperse the scum on the top. Ladle the jam, or pour it from a small heatproof liquid measuring cup into sterilized jars through a canning funnel.

package directions to make sure the quantities are correct for that particular brand; pectin types are not interchangeable.

The pectin in fruit makes the jam set, but it is the sugar that acts as the preservative. For jam and preserves recipes, granulated sugar is a good choice. (If other types of recipes call for superfine sugar, you can susbstitute it with the same amount of granulated sugar processed in a food processor for 1 minute.)

Testing for setting

Getting the temperature right is crucial; just as a jam can be ruined if too runny, overcooking can destroy the color and flavor, producing a much darker color and too firm a consistency. If you are not using pectin, begin testing after 10 minutes and then at 2–3-minute intervals. There are three ways to check the setting point, but you will be able to tell if it is almost there because the jam will begin to lose height

as it boils in the pan, will make more noise, and large bubbles will begin to form. When you think it is ready, remove the pan from the heat and use one of the three tests.

Flake test: Gently stir, then lift the spoon out of the pan and hold so that it is vertical. If the jam forms a large blob or flake that slowly drops from the spoon, it is ready. If it runs off in a thin stream, it isn't ready; heat again and retry after a few minutes.

Saucer test: Place two or three saucers in the refrigerator before you begin jam making, so that they get cold (or put them into the freezer if you forget when you begin dissolving the sugar). Remove from the heat when you think the jam is nearly ready, drop 2 teaspoons of the hot jam onto the cold plate, let cool for a minute or two, then run your index finger through the jam. If the top wrinkles and a path remains briefly, it is ready.

Thermometer test: Perhaps the most fail-safe method, put a candy thermometer into the spread without touching the pan; it should read 8 degrees above boiling point. At sea level, that is 220°F, but subtract 2 degrees for each 1,000 feet above sea level; for example, 214°F at 3,000 feet. Stir the jam before testing the temperature, because it can be hotter in the center.

What can go wrong?

Follow the recipes exactly; for example, too much or too little pectin or citric acid can mean the preserves do not set properly.

Jam is runny

You may not have let the jam boil long enough. If still soft the next day, pour the jam back into a pan and boil again. If you are unsure of the setting point, use several different ways to test the set; first the flake test, with the thermometer to see if the jam is nearly ready, then with the saucer test. To remake a soft jelly that did not have enough lemon juice or pectin added, for each 4 cups of jelly, add 2 tablespoons of lemon juice and boil for 3–4 minutes before canning again; or add ¾ cup sugar, 2 tablespoons liquid pectin, and 2 tablespoons lemon juice after bringing the jelly to a boil over high heat, then return to a boil for 1 minute before canning.

Jam is dark and set

Getting the setting point absolutely right can be difficult and it is tempting to overcook. The longer the jam cooks, the darker it will become and the more liquid will disappear through evaporation, producing a much firmer set. As a rough guide, the finished jam should make 1½–2 times the amount of sugar used.

Jelly looks cloudy

It is important to cook the fruit over low heat until softened; don't try to speed up the process by turning up the heat. Likewise, after the cooked fruit and juice is spooned into the jelly bag, don't squeeze the bag because you will lose clarity in the finished jelly. Allow for a minimum of 3–4 hours, preferably overnight, to drip through the bag.

Sugar has crystallized in the jar

When adding sugar, always heat gently, stirring occasionally, before bringing to a boil and a set, or this can cause crystallization and the jam may be crunchy. Or there could be too much sugar and the preserve was overboiled.

Jam tastes a little like wine

The fruit has fermented. This could be caused by insufficient cooking before the sugar was added, or insufficient sugar added. Or the fruit was overripe when used. If you catch this in the early stages, transfer any unopened jars to the refrigerator or freezer to stop further fermentation. If freezing, transfer the contents of the jars to plastic containers with lids, leaving a headspace of ½ inch because the jam expands during freezing. Jam requires 60 percent sugar if it is to keep well.

Surface of jam has a layer of mold

The jar was not sealed correctly. Always follow the directions for canning the jars precisely. Dispose of the jam.

the canning process

By heating preserves in a hot-water canner or pressure canner, any potentially dangerous microorganisms, such as molds, yeasts, and bacteria, are destroyed and the contents are hermetically sealed in—they are airtight. High-acid foods, which include most fruits, such as apples, apricots, blackberries, gooseberries, lemons, peaches, pears, plums, and sour cherries, as well as pickles and sauerkraut, can be processed in a boiling-water canner at 212°F. Low-acid foods, which includes most vegetables, needs processing in a pressure canner at 240°F. Tomatoes and figs are borderline, but by adding an acidic ingredient, such as vinegar or lemon juice, they can be safely processed in a boiling-water canner.

Canning jars and lids

The only recommended type of canning jar is the mason-style jar that comes with a two-part lid with screw band. It is available in ½ pint, 1 pint, 1½ pints, 1 quart, and ½ gallon sizes, with 1 pint sizes being common. The jars and screw bands can be reused, but the lids should be used only once.

Clean empty jars before use and rinse well to remove any detergents, by hand or dishwasher. Preheat the jars and keep them warm while the preserves are being made by keeping them submerged in simmering water at 180°F in a stockpot or boiling-water canner. Or put them on a regular cycle in a dishwasher, keeping them in the closed dishwasher until the jars are needed for filling. The lids, but not the screw bands, also need to be heated in a saucepan of simmering water at 180°F until needed. A magnetic wand—a stick with a magnet on one end—is useful for retrieving lids from hot water.

If jams, jellies, or pickles will be processed for less than 10 minutes, the jars need sterillizing. After cleaning them thoroughly, put the jars, right-side up, in a boiling-water canner with the rack in the bottom, then add enough water to have 1 inch above the top of the jars. Bring the water to a boil and boil for 10 minutes, plus 1 minute per every 1,000 feet of elevation. Reduce the heat and keep the jars in the canner until needed, removing one at a time.

Filling the jars

Working with one jar at a time, use a jar lifter or large tongs to remove a jar from the water and place it on a protected surface, such as a wooden cutting board or dish towel. Using a funnel, add the preserves to the jar, leaving the headspace indicated in the recipe—this

ALTITUDE ADJUSTMENT TIMES

ALTITUDE	BOILING WATER PROCESSING TIME
0–1,000 feet	time given in recipe
1,001–3,000 feet	add 5 minutes
3,001–6,000 feet	add 10 minutes
6,001–8,000 feet	add 15 minutes
8,001–10,000 feet	add 20 minutes

Processing the jars

Lower the jars into the boiling-water canner (or pressure canner) and onto the rack, using a jar lifter or tongs. Add enough water to cover the jars by 1 inch, then cover with a lid and bring to a rolling boil. The length of boiling time depends on the recipe and where you live. The higher the elevation where you are, the lower the temperature at which water boils. If you are using a boiling-water canner, you need to adjust the amount of time the preserves are heated to destroy any micro-oganisms. The times in the recipes are for sea level, so if you live above 1,000 feet—check with your county cooperative extension office if you are unsure—you need to increase the length of time as indicated. (If you are using a pressure canner, the gauge will need to be adjusted—check the manufacturer's instruc-tions.) Turn off the heat, remove the lid, and let rest for 5 minutes before removing the jars.

Checking the seals and storing

Let cool undisturbed for 24 hours. Remove the screw bands (they are no longer needed) and check the seals. At eye level, the lid should look curved down in the center. If the lid springs up when you press down on it, it is not sealed. Store in the refrigerator and use within several days, or reprocess within 24 hours. Most canned preserves can be stored for up to a year if kept in a cool, dark place, away from heat or light. Once any jar of preserve is opened, store in the refrigerator.

is a gap above the contents, ¼ inch for fruit spreads and ½ inch for tomatoes, chutneys, relishes, and pickles. Too much headspace and the jar won't seal properly; but too little, and the contents can overflow. Using a plastic or rubber spatula, stir the contents in the jar to remove any air bubbles that could ruin the preserves.

Remove any drips from the rim and threads of the jar with a damp paper towel, center a lid on the jar, position the screw band, and tighten, following the manufacturer's instructions.

jams, preserves, & conserves

strawberry jam

Makes **five to six 1-pint jars**
Preparation time **10 minutes**
Cooking time **16 minutes**
(not including canning time)

2 quarts **strawberries**,
 hulled, halved, or quartered,
 depending on size
 (about 9 cups)
3 tablespoons freshly
 squeezed **lemon juice**
 (about 1½ lemons)
1 (1¾-oz) box **powdered
 pectin**
7½ cups **granulated sugar**
1 tablespoon **butter** (optional)

Prepare a boiling-water canner (see pages 16–17). Sterilize the jars and lids. Set the screw bands aside.

Add half the strawberries to a large saucepan and crush them coarsely with a vegetable masher. Add the lemon juice and pectin, and mix until the pectin has dissolved. Add the remaining strawberries and heat gently for 15 minutes, until the fruit has softened.

Bring to a boil, then add the sugar, return to a full rolling boil, and boil rapidly for 1 minute. Skim with a skimming spoon or stir in butter, if needed.

Ladle into the sterilized jars, working with one at a time. Fill each jar to ¼ inch from the top. Using a plastic spatula, disperse any air bubbles, then clean the rim and threads of the jar before covering with a lid and securing with a screw band. Repeat with the remaining jars.

Process the filled jars in a boiling-water canner for 5 minutes at sea level (see page 16). Let cool, clean the jars, and label before storing.

For strawberry & lavender jam, stir 3 teaspoons dried lavender petals into the cooked jam after skimming.

spiced plum preserves

Makes **eight to ten ½-pint jars**
Preparation time **25 minutes**
Cooking time **50–55 minutes**
(not including canning time)

1½ quarts **just-ripe plums**
   (about 3 lb), halved
   and pitted
grated rind and juice of
   1 orange
1¼ cups **water**
1 **cinnamon stick**, halved
1 teaspoon **whole cloves**
7½ cups **granulated sugar**
1 tablespoon **butter** (optional)

Prepare a boiling-water canner (see pages 16–17). Sterilize the jars and lids. Set the screw bands aside.

Add the plums, orange rind and juice, and measured water to a large saucepan. Tie the cinnamon stick and cloves in cheesecloth, then add to the pan. Cover and cook gently for 30 minutes, until the plums are softened.

Pour the sugar into the pan and heat gently, stirring occasionally, until dissolved. Bring to a boil, then boil rapidly until setting point is reached (20–25 minutes). Discard the bag of spices. Skim with a skimming spoon or stir in the butter, if needed.

Ladle into the sterilized jars, working with one at a time. Fill each jar to ¼ inch from the top. Using a plastic spatula, disperse any air bubbles, then clean the rim and threads of the jar before covering with a lid and securing with a screw band. Repeat with the remaining jars.

Process the filled jars in a boiling-water canner for 5 minutes at sea level (see page 16). Let cool, clean the jars, and label before storing.

To serve, this jam is delicious in sweet bread rolls with whipped cream.

For spiced greengage preserves, make as above using 1½ quarts (3 lb) halved and pitted greengages instead of the plums.

cranberry & apple preserves

Makes **eight 1-pint jars**
Preparation time **25 minutes**
Cooking time **40–45 minutes**
(not including canning time)

3 cups **fresh** or **frozen
cranberries**
3 lb **cooking apples,**
peeled, cored, and diced
(about 14 cups)
grated rind and juice of
2 **oranges**, shells reserved
10 cups **granulated sugar**
1 tablespoon **butter** (optional)

Prepare a boiling-water canner (see pages 16–17) and heat the cleaned jars and lids in simmering water. Set the screw bands aside.

Add the cranberries, apples, and orange rind to a large saucepan, with the orange shells and any seeds tied in cheesecloth. Make the orange juice up to 1 ¼ cups with water, then add to the pan. Cover and simmer gently for 30 minutes, stirring occasionally, until the fruit is tender.

Pour the sugar into the pan and heat gently, stirring occasionally, until dissolved. Bring to a boil, then boil rapidly until setting point is reached (10–15 minutes). Squeeze the cheesecloth between two wooden spoons to extract as much juice as possible, then discard. Skim with a skimming spoon or stir in the butter, if needed.

Ladle into the warmed jars, working with one at a time. Fill each jar to ¼ inch from the top. Using a plastic spatula, disperse any air bubbles, then clean the rim and threads of the jar before covering with a lid and securing with a screw band. Repeat with the remaining jars.

Process the filled jars in a boiling-water canner for 10 minutes at sea level (see page 16). Let cool, clean the jars, and label before storing.

To serve, try on buttered, toasted bagels.

For blackberry, apple, & cinnamon preserves, follow the recipe above, but substitute 4 cups blackberries for the cranberries, and use a 3-inch cinnamon stick, halved, and the grated rind of 2 lemons instead of the orange shell and seeds. Replace the orange juice with the juice of 2 lemons.

blueberry & honey jam

Makes **about three ½-pint jars**
Preparation time **10 minutes**
Cooking time **16 minutes**
(not including canning time)

4 cups **blueberries**
⅔ cup **water**
juice of 1 **lemon**
1 (1¾-oz) box **powdered
  pectin**
2 cups **granulated sugar**
½ cup **honey**
1 tablespoon **butter** (optional)

Prepare a boiling-water canner (see pages 16–17).
Sterilize the jars and lids. Set the screw bands aside.

Add the blueberries to a large saucepan and crush
with a wooden spoon or vegetable masher, then add
the measured water and cook gently for 10 minutes,
until softened. Add the lemon juice and pectin, and
mix well until the pectin dissolves.

Bring to a boil, then add the sugar and honey, return
to a full rolling boil, and boil rapidly for 1 minute. Skim
with a skimming spoon or stir in butter, if needed.

Ladle into the sterilized jars, working with one at a
time. Fill each jar to ¼ inch from the top. Using a plastic
spatula, disperse any air bubbles, then clean the rim and
threads of the jar before covering with a lid and securing
with a screw band. Repeat with the remaining jars.

Process the filled jars in a boiling-water canner for
5 minutes at sea level (see page 16). Let cool, clean
the jars, and label before storing.

To serve, a spoonful of this jam and a spoonful of
whipped cream makes a tasty addition to oatmeal.

For raspberry & honey jam, follow the recipe above
but substitute 5 cups raspberries for the blueberries.

black & red currant jam

Makes **about eight ½-pint jars**
Preparation time **15 minutes**
Cooking time **40–50 minutes**
(not including canning time)

5 cups fresh **red currants**
5 cups fresh **black currants**
1 cup **water**
5 cups **granulated sugar**
1 tablespoon **butter** (optional)

Prepare a boiling-water canner (see pages 16–17). Sterilize the jars and lids. Set the screw bands aside.

Strip the currants from the stems, then add to a large saucepan. Break up the fruit with a wooden spoon or vegetable masher, then add the measured water. Cover and cook gently for 20–30 minutes, until the fruit is soft.

Pour the sugar into the pan and heat gently, stirring occasionally, until dissolved. Bring to a boil, then boil rapidly, stirring occasionally, until setting point is reached (about 20 minutes). Skim with a skimming spoon or stir in butter, if needed.

Ladle into the sterilized jars, working with one at a time. Fill each jar to ¼ inch from the top. Using a plastic spatula, disperse any air bubbles, then clean the rim and threads of the jar before covering with a lid and securing with a screw band. Repeat with the remaining jars.

Process the filled jars in a boiling-water canner for 5 minutes at sea level (see page 16). Let cool, clean the jars, and label before storing.

To serve, this jam is perfect for spooning over individual pavlovas topped with whipped cream.

For elderberry & blackberry jam, prepare a boiling-water canner and jars. Strip 3¼ cups elderberries from their stems and add to a large saucepan with 2⅔ cups blackberries and ⅔ cup water. Cover and cook for 20–30 minutes, stirring and mashing with a vegetable masher, until the fruit is soft. Add ¼ cup lemon juice and 5 cups granulated sugar and continue as above.

fresh fig & blackberry preserves

Makes **about four ½-pint jars**
Preparation time **20 minutes**
Cooking time **35 minutes**
(not including canning time)

2⅔ cups **blackberries**
 (about 1 lb)
9 **figs** (about 1 lb), quartered
1¼ cups **water**
2 **cinnamon sticks**, halved
5 cups **granulated sugar**
juice of 1 **lemon**
1 tablespoon **butter** (optional)

Prepare a boiling-water canner (see pages 16–17). Sterilize the jars and lids. Set the screw bands aside.

Add the blackberries and figs to a large saucepan. Pour in the measured water, then add the cinnamon sticks. Bring to a simmer, then simmer, uncovered, for about 10 minutes, until the fruit is just beginning to soften.

Pour the sugar into the pan and add the lemon juice. Heat gently, stirring occasionally, until the sugar has dissolved. Bring to a boil, then boil rapidly until setting point is reached (about 25 minutes). Skim with a skimming spoon or stir in butter, if needed.

Ladle into the sterilized jars, working with one at a time. Fill each jar to ¼ inch from the top. Using a plastic spatula, disperse any air bubbles, then clean the rim and threads of the jar before covering with a lid and securing with a screw band. Repeat with the remaining jars.

Process the filled jars in a boiling-water canner for 5 minutes at sea level (see page 16). Let cool, clean the jars, and label before storing.

For gingered blackberry & fig preserves, omit the cinnamon sticks and add a 1½-inch piece of ginger root, peeled and finely chopped.

orchard fruit preserves

Makes **about five ½-pint jars**
Preparation time **25 minutes**
Cooking time **40–45 minutes**
(not including canning time)

10 **plums** (about 1 lb),
   halved and pitted
3 **pears** (about 1 lb),
   quartered, cored, peeled,
   and diced
3 **cooking apples**
   (about 1 lb), quartered,
   cored, peeled, and diced
1¼ cups **water**
7½ cups **granulated sugar**
1 tablespoon **butter** (optional)

Prepare a boiling-water canner (see pages 16–17). Sterilize the jars and lids. Set the screw bands aside.

Add the fruit to a large saucepan with the measured water. Cover and cook gently for 20 minutes, stirring occasionally, until the fruit is just beginning to soften.

Pour the sugar into the pan and heat gently, stirring occasionally, until dissolved. Bring to a boil, then boil rapidly until setting point is reached (20–25 minutes). Skim with a skimming spoon or stir in butter, if needed.

Ladle into the sterilized jars, working with one at a time. Fill each jar to ¼ inch from the top. Using a plastic spatula, disperse any air bubbles, then clean the rim and threads of the jar before covering with a lid and securing with a screw band. Repeat with the remaining jars.

Process the filled jars in a boiling-water canner for 5 minutes at sea level (see page 16). Let cool, clean the jars, and label before storing.

To serve, this jam can be used as the filling between 2 shortbread cookies—the top layer having a small heart shape cut out before baking.

For apple & blackberry preserves, prepare a boiling-water canner and sterlize the jars and lids. Cook 4–5 (about 1 ½ lb) cooking apples, quartered, cored, peeled, and diced, with 5 cups blackberries in 1 ¼ cups water, then continue as above.

pineapple & passion fruit preserves

Makes **about four to five**
½-pint jars
Preparation time **15 minutes**
Cooking time **1 hour**
40 minutes–1 hour
50 minutes
(not including canning time)

1 large ripe **pineapple**,
including leaves
4–5 **cooking apples**
(about 1½ lb), coarsely
chopped
6 **passion fruit**, quartered
5 cups **water**
7½ cups **granulated sugar**
juice of 2 large **lemons**
1 tablespoon **butter** (optional)

Prepare a boiling-water canner (see pages 16–17) and heat the cleaned jars and lids in simmering water. Set the screw bands aside.

Peel the pineapple and coarsely chop the peel with the leaves. Put the chopped peel and leaves into a saucepan with the apples and passion fruit and add the measured water. Bring to a boil, reduce the heat, cover the pan, and simmer for 1 hour. Meanwhile, chop the flesh, cutting the core more finely than the soft part of the fruit. Set aside.

Press the cooked pulp through a fine strainer, pour the puree back into the pan, and add the fresh pineapple. Bring slowly to a boil, reduce the heat to a simmer, cover, and cook the fruit for 30 minutes, until tender.

Add the sugar and lemon juice and cook over low heat, stirring continuously, until the sugar has dissolved. Bring to a boil, then boil rapidly until setting point is reached (10–20 minutes). Remove from the heat and skim with a skimming spoon or stir in butter, if needed.

Ladle into the warmed jars, working with one at a time. Fill each jar to ¼ inch from the top. Using a plastic spatula, disperse any air bubbles, then clean the rim and threads of the jar before covering with a lid and securing with a screw band. Repeat with the remaining jars.

Process the filled jars in a boiling-water canner for 15 minutes at sea level (see page 16). Let cool, clean the jars, and label before storing.

For gingered pineapple & raisin preserves, cook as above, adding a 1½-inch piece of peeled, finely chopped ginger root and ⅔ cup golden raisins along with the sugar.

plum & zucchini preserves

Makes **about six ½-pint jars**
Preparation time **25 minutes**
Cooking time **35–40 minutes**
(not including canning time)

1 **zucchini** (1½–1¾ lb),
  peeled, halved, seeded,
  and diced
1½ quarts **just-ripe plums**
  (about 3 lb), quartered
  and pitted
1¾ cups **blackberries**
1¼ cups **water**
7½ cups **granulated sugar**
1 tablespoon **butter** (optional)

Prepare a boiling-water canner (see pages 16–17).
Sterilize the jars and lids. Set the screw bands aside.

Add the zucchini, plums, and blackberries to a large
saucepan with the measured water, then cover and
cook for 20 minutes, until the fruits are just tender.

Pour the sugar into the pan and heat gently, stirring
occasionally, until dissolved. Bring to a boil, then boil
rapidly until setting point is reached (15–20 minutes).
Skim with a skimming spoon or stir in butter, if needed.

Ladle into the sterilized jars, working with one at a
time. Fill each jar to ¼ inch from the top. Using a plastic
spatula, disperse any air bubbles, then clean the rim and
threads of the jar before covering with a lid and securing
with a screw band. Repeat with the remaining jars.

Process the filled jars in a boiling-water canner for
5 minutes at sea level (see page 16). Let cool, clean
the jars, and label before storing.

To serve, this jam is delicious simply eaten with bread
and butter.

For apple, zucchini, & ginger preserves, follow
the recipe as above, but in place of the plums add
3½ lb cooking apples, quartered, cored, and diced,
to 1 prepared zucchni, and add the grated rind and juice
of 2 lemons and ⅓ cup drained and finely chopped
preserved ginger in place of the blackberries.

raspberry & red currant preserves

Makes **about four ½-pint jars**
Preparation time **5 minutes**
Cooking time **30–40 minutes**
(not including canning time)

4 cups **raspberries**
4 cups **red currants**
1¼ cups **water**
juice of 2 **lemons**
5 cups **granulated sugar**
1 tablespoon **butter** (optional)

Prepare a boiling-water canner (see pages 16–17). Sterilize the jars and lids. Set the screw bands aside.

Add the fruit to a suacepan with the measured water. Bring to a boil, then reduce the heat and cover the pan. Simmer for 20–30 minutes, until the red currants are really tender.

Add the lemon juice and sugar and stir over low heat until the sugar has completely dissolved. Increase the heat and bring to a boil, then boil rapidly until setting point is reached (10–20 minutes). Remove the pan from the heat and skim with a skimming spoon or stir in butter, if needed.

Ladle into the sterilized jars, working with one at a time. Fill each jar to ¼ inch from the top. Using a plastic spatula, disperse any air bubbles, then clean the rim and threads of the jar before covering with a lid and securing with a screw band. Repeat with the remaining jars.

Process the filled jars in a boiling-water canner for 5 minutes at sea level (see page 16). Let cool, clean the jars, and label before storing.

To serve, spoon over split scones or other sweet breads, cookies, or cake topped with whipped cream.

For gooseberry & strawberry preserves, prepare a boiling-water canner and the jars and lids. Add 3¼ cups gooseberries to a saucepan with ⅔ cup water, cover, and cook gently for 15 minutes, until soft. Add 2⅔ cups strawberries, cook for 10 minutes, mashing thm with a vegetable masher, until soft. Add 5 cups granulated sugar, then continue as above. (No need to add lemon juice.)

mango & passion fruit preserves

Makes **about five ½-pint jars**
Preparation time **30 minutes**
Cooking time **18–30 minutes**
(not including canning time)

3 large ripe **mangoes**
(about 4 lb), peeled, pitted,
and diced
grated rind and juice of
3 large **limes**
½ cup **water**
5 cups **granulated sugar**
3 **passion fruit**, halved

Prepare a boiling-water canner (see pages 16–17) and heat the cleaned jars and lids in simmering water. Set the screw bands aside.

Add the diced mango flesh to a saucepan with the lime juice and measured water. Cook, uncovered, over low heat for 8–10 minutes, stirring occasionally, until the mango is soft.

Add the lime rind and sugar and heat gently, stirring occasionally, until the sugar has completely dissolved. Bring to a boil, then boil rapidly until setting point is reached (10–20 minutes). Turn off the heat, scoop the passion fruit seeds from the fruit with a teaspoon, and stir into the jam.

Ladle into the warmed jars, working with one at a time. Fill each jar to ¼ inch from the top. Using a plastic spatula, disperse any air bubbles, then clean the rim and threads of the jar before covering with a lid and securing with a screw band. Repeat with the remaining jars.

Process the filled jars in a boiling-water canner for 10 minutes at sea level (see page 16). Let cool, clean the jars, and label before storing.

For papaya & lime preserves, replace the mangoes with 3 large ripe papayas, halved and seeded, then peeled and diced, and use 6 large limes instead of 3 limes. Mash the papaya from time to time as it cooks with the lime rind and juice and water, and continue as above.

cherry & raspberry preserves

Makes **about four to five
½-pint jars**
Preparation time **20 minutes**
Cooking time **16 minutes**
(not including canning time)

3 (10-oz) packages **frozen
pitted cherries**
3 cups **fresh raspberries**
1 (1¾-oz) box **powdered
pectin**
5 cups **granulated sugar**
1 tablespoon **butter** (optional)

Prepare a boiling-water canner (see pages 16–17).
Sterilize the jars and lids. Set the screw bands aside.

Add the cherries and the raspberries to a large
saucepan, cover, and cook gently for 10 minutes,
stirring occasionally until the juice runs and the fruits
begin to soften. Add the pectin and mix until the pectin
has completely dissolved.

Bring to a boil, then add the sugar, return to a full rolling
boil, and boil rapidly for 1 minute. Skim with a skimming
spoon or stir in butter, if needed.

Ladle into the sterilized jars, working with one at a
time. Fill each jar to ¼ inch from the top. Using a plastic
spatula, disperse any air bubbles, then clean the rim and
threads of the jar before covering with a lid and securing
with a screw band. Repeat with the remaining jars.

Process the filled jars in a boiling-water canner for
5 minutes at sea level (see page 16). Let cool, clean
the jars, and label before storing.

For blueberry & raspberry preserves, omit the frozen
cherries and add 5½ cups frozen blueberries. Cook with
the fresh raspberries and continue as above.

chestnut jam with whiskey

Makes **about two ½-pint jars**
Preparation time **15 minutes**
Cooking time **50 minutes**
(not including canning time)

4 (5-oz) pouches **cooked,
    peeled chestnuts**
1 **vanilla bean**
1¾ cups firmly packed **light
    brown sugar**
2 tablespoons **whiskey**

Prepare a boiling-water canner (see pages 16–17) and heat the cleaned jars and lids in simmering water. Set the screw bands aside.

Put the chestnuts and vanilla bean into a saucepan and add water to just cover them. Bring to a boil, reduce the heat, cover the pan, and simmer for 30 minutes. Remove the vanilla bean and set aside, then strain and reserve the cooking liquid. Puree the chestnuts in a food processor or blender, adding a little reserved liquid, if needed.

Add the chestnut puree back to the pan. Slice the vanilla bean lengthwise and scrape the seeds into the pan. Add the sugar and ⅓ cup of cooking liquid and stir to blend. Bring to a boil, stirring often, and cook for 5 minutes, or until thick. Remove from the heat and add the whiskey.

Ladle into the warmed jars, working with one at a time. Fill each jar to ¼ inch from the top. Using a plastic spatula, disperse any air bubbles, then clean the rim and threads of the jar before covering with a lid and securing with a screw band. Repeat with the remaining jars.

Process the filled jars in a boiling-water canner for 10 minutes at sea level (see page 16). Let cool, clean the jars, and label before storing.

To serve, layer spoonfuls of jam in small glasses with honey-flavored yogurt.

For chestnut, cinnamon, & orange jam, follow the recipe as above, but omit the vanilla and mix the grated rind and juice of 1 large orange and 1 teaspoon ground cinnamon with the chestnut puree, and substitute 2 tablespoons Grand Marnier or Cointreau for the whiskey.

strawberry champagne preserves

Makes **about five to six
½-pint jars**
Preparation time **10 minutes,
plus standing**
Cooking time **16 minutes**
(not including canning time)

2 quarts **strawberries**, hulled
or quartered, depending on
size (about 9 cups)
⅔ cup **dry champagne** or
sparkling white wine
1½ teaspoons **citric acid**
1 (1¾-oz) box **powdered
pectin**
7½ cups **granulated sugar**
1 tablespon **butter** (optional)

Prepare a boiling-water canner (see pages 16–17).
Sterilize the jars and lids. Set the screw bands aside.

Add half the strawberries to a saucepan and crush
them coarsely with a vegetable masher. Add the
remaining strawberries, the champagne or wine, and
citric acid and heat gently for 10 minutes, stirring
continuously. Add the pectin and mix until the pectin
is completely dissolved.

Bring to a boil, then add the sugar, return to a full rolling
boil, and boil rapidly for 1 minute. Skim with a skimming
spoon or stir in butter, if needed.

Ladle into the sterilized jars, working with one at a
time. Fill each jar to ¼ inch from the top. Using a plastic
spatula, disperse any air bubbles, then clean the rim and
threads of the jar before covering with a lid and securing
with a screw band. Repeat with the remaining jars.

Process the filled jars in a boiling-water canner for
5 minutes at sea level (see page 16). Let cool, clean
the jars, and label before storing.

To serve, spread over hot, buttered English muffins.

For lychee & strawberry preserves, follow the recipe
as above, but add 5 cups peeled and pitted lychees to a
saucepan with 5 cups hulled strawberries and coarsely
crush with a with a vegetable masher, omitting the
remaining strawberries, and replace the champagne
with the same quantity of water.

peach & vanilla preserves

Makes **about three 1-pint jars**
Preparation time **20 minutes**
Cooking time **21 minutes**
(not including canning time)

6 **ripe peaches** (about 2 lb),
   halved, pitted, and diced
juice of 1 large **lemon**
1 **vanilla bean**
1 (1¾-oz) box **powdered
   pectin**
5 cups **granulated sugar**
1 tablespoon **butter** (optional)

Prepare a boiling-water canner (see pages 16–17).
Sterilize the jars and lids. Set the screw bands aside.

Add the peaches and lemon juice to a large saucepan.
Slit the vanilla bean lengthwise, then scrape out the
seeds and add to the pan. Cut the bean into thin
strips and add to the pan. Cook gently, uncovered, for
20 minutes, until the peaches are tender. Add the pectin
and mix until the pectin is completely dissolved.

Bring to a boil, then add the sugar, return to a full rolling
boil, and boil rapidly for 1 minute. Skim with a skimming
spoon or stir in butter, if needed.

Ladle into the sterilized jars, working with one at a
time. Fill each jar to ¼ inch from the top. Using a plastic
spatula, disperse any air bubbles, then clean the rim and
threads of the jar before covering with a lid and securing
with a screw band. Repeat with the remaining jars.

Process the filled jars in a boiling-water canner for
5 minutes at sea level (see page 16). Let cool, clean
the jars, and label before storing.

For apricot & vodka preserves, follow the recipe as
above, but use 8 halved, pitted, and diced fresh apricots
(about 2 lb) instead of the peaches, and stir in ¼ cup
vodka with the sugar.

pineapple & kiwi preserves

Makes **about three ½-pint jars**
Preparation time **25 minutes**
Cooking time **25–35 minutes**
(not including canning time)

1 large **pineapple**, trimmed,
   peeled, and cored
grated rind of 2 **limes**
½ cup freshly squeezed
   lime juice (about 3 limes)
4 **kiwis**, peeled and
   thinly sliced
3¾ cups **granulated sugar**
1 tablespoon **butter** (optional)

Prepare a boiling-water canner (see pages 16–17) and heat the cleaned jars and lids in simmering water. Set the screw bands aside.

Dice half the pineapple, then finely chop the remainder in a food processor. Add the diced and crushed pineapple, lime rind, and lime juice to a suacepan, then cover and cook gently for 10 minutes. Add the kiwis and cook for 5 minutes, until the fruit has softened.

Pour in the sugar and heat gently, stirring occasionally, until dissolved. Bring to a boil, then boil rapidly until setting point is reached (10–20 minutes). Skim with a skimming spoon or stir in butter, if needed.

Ladle into the warmed jars, working with one at a time. Fill each jar to ¼ inch from the top. Using a plastic spatula, disperse any air bubbles, then clean the rim and threads of the jar before covering with a lid and securing with a screw band. Repeat with the remaining jars.

Process the filled jars in a boiling-water canner for 15 minutes at sea level (see page 16). Let cool, clean the jars, and label before storing.

To serve, this preserve is delicious with toast and butter.

For pineapple & pomegranate preserves, follow the recipe as above, but omit the kiwis and stir the seeds from 1 pomegranate into the preserve just as it comes up to setting point.

peach melba preserves

Makes **about seven**
 ½-pint jars
Preparation time **25 minutes**
Cooking time **16 minutes**
(not including canning time)

3 lb **peaches**, halved, pitted,
 and diced (about 9 cups)
grated rind and juice of
 2 lemons
¾ cup plus 2 tbsp **water**
2 cups **raspberries**
1 (1¾-oz) box **powdered**
 pectin
8¾ cups **granulated sugar**
1 tablespoon **butter** (optional)

Prepare a boiling-water canner (see pages 16–17).
Sterilize the jars and lids. Set the screw bands aside.

Add the peaches to a large saucepan with the lemon rind
and juice and measured water. Cover and cook gently
for 15 minutes, until the peaches are just softened. Add
the raspberries and pectin, and mix until the pectin is
completely dissolved.

Bring to a boil, then add the sugar, return to a full rolling
boil, and boil rapidly for 1 minute. Skim with a skimming
spoon or stir in butter, if needed.

Ladle into the sterilized jars, working with one at a
time. Fill each jar to ¼ inch from the top. Using a plastic
spatula, disperse any air bubbles, then clean the rim and
threads of the jar before covering with a lid and securing
with a screw band. Repeat with the remaining jars.

Process the filled jars in a boiling-water canner for
5 minutes at sea level (see page 16). Let cool, clean
the jars, and label before storing.

To serve, these preserves go well with vanilla ice cream
and sliced peaches.

For peach jam, make as above using 3½ lb peaches
(about 11 cups) instead of the peaches and raspberries.

quick tropical fruit preserves

Makes **four to five ½-pint jars**
Preparation time **20 minutes**
Cooking time **16 minutes**

3 (16-oz) bags **frozen
    prepared tropical fruit**,
    including pineapple,
    mango, papaya, kiwi, and
    pomegranate seeds
grated rind and juice of
    2 large **limes**
1 (1¾-oz) box **pectin**
5 cups **granulated sugar**
1 tablespoon **butter** (optional)

Sterilize the jars and lids (see pages 16–17), setting the screw bands aside, or sterilize freezer containers.

Add the frozen fruit to a large saucepan with the lime rind and juice. Cover and cook gently for 10 minutes, stirring occasionally, until the juices begin to run.

Coarsely chop the fruit while still in the pan, using a knife and fork, if the pieces are large. Add the pectin and mix until completely dissolved.

Bring to a boil, then add the sugar, return to a full rolling boil, and boil rapidly for 1 minute. Skim with a skimming spoon or stir in butter, if needed. Let cool for 10 minutes so that the fruit doesn't rise in the jars.

Ladle into sterilized, dry jars, leaving a ½-inch headspace at the top and packing down well. Disperse any air pockets with a plastic spatula. Cover with the lids and let stand at room temperature for 24 hours.

Store in the refrigerator for up to 3 weeks or the freezer for up to a year. Once open, store in the refrigerator and use within a few days.

For quick mixed berry preserves, use 3 (1-lb) bags mixed frozen berries and cherries, cook with the grated rind and juice of 2 lemons, then add sugar and continue as above.

no-cook strawberry jam

Makes **about three ½-pint jars**
Preparation time **20 minutes,
plus standing and freezing**

3½ cups hulled and sliced
strawberries (about 1¼ lb)
5 cups **superfine sugar**
¼ cup freshly squeezed **lemon
juice** (about 2 lemons)
2 (3-oz) pouches **liquid pectin**

Sterilize the jars and lids, or sterilize freezer containers.

Crush the strawberries with a vegetable masher, or by blending briefly in a food processor, using the pulse setting so that there are pieces of strawberry rather than a fine puree. Add to a large bowl and stir in the sugar, then cover and let stand for 1½–2 hours, stirring occasionally, until the sugar has dissolved.

Stir in the lemon juice, then add the pectin and continue stirring for 2 minutes. Let cool for 10 minutes so that the fruit doesn't rise in the jars.

Ladle into sterilized, dry jars, leaving a ½-inch headspace at the top and packing down well. Disperse any air pockets with a plastic spatula. Cover with the lids and let stand at room temperature for 24 hours.

Store in the refrigerator for up to 3 weeks or the freezer for up to a year. Once open, store in the refrigerator and use within a few days.

For no-cook raspberry jam, follow the recipe as above, but using 4 cups raspberries, coarsely crushed, instead of the strawberries.

reduced-sugar apricot preserves

Makes **about two ½-pint jars**
Preparation time **25 minutes**
Cooking time **35–40 minutes**

5 **Pippin, McIntosh, Cortland,**
   or Fuji apples (about
   1½ lb), quartered, cored,
   peeled, and diced
2 cups diced **dried apricots**
2 cups **water**
2 tablespoons **honey**

Sterilize the jars and lids.

Add the apples, apricots, and measured water to a medium saucepan, then drizzle the honey over the fruits. Cover and cook gently for 30 minutes, stirring and mashing the fruit occasionally with a fork, until soft.

Remove the lid and cook for another 5–10 minutes, stirring frequently, until thick and jamlike. Because this jam has only a little honey, it is more like a chutney in consistency and doesn't need to be tested for setting.

Ladle into sterilized, dry jars, packing down well and leaving a ½-inch headspace at the top. Disperse any air pockets with a plastic spatula. Cover with the lids, let cool, and store in the refrigerator for up to 10 days.

For reduced-sugar apricot, date, & apple preserves, follow the recipe as above, but reduce the dried apricots to 1 cup, add 1 cup diced dates with the apricots, and add 2 teaspoons ground cinnamon with the honey.

green grape preserves

Makes **about two ½-pint jars**
Preparation time **20 minutes**
Cooking time **10–20 minutes**
(not including canning time)

6½ cups **seedless green grapes** (about 2 lb)
grated rind and juice of
1 **lemon**
6 tablespoons **water**
2½ cups **granulated sugar**
1 tablespoon **butter** (optional)

Prepare a boiling-water canner (see pages 16–17). Sterilize the jars and lids. Set the screw bands aside.

Wash the grapes and pick off the bunch, carefully removing the stems. Add the fruit to a medium saucepan with the lemon rind and juice and the measured water. Cover and simmer gently for 10 minutes, until the juices have run and the fruit has softened.

Coarsely mash the grapes with a vegetable masher, then add the sugar and cook gently, stirring occasionally, until the sugar has completely dissolved. Bring to a boil and cook until setting point is reached (10–20 minutes). Skim with a skimming spoon or stir in butter, if needed.

Ladle into the sterilized jars, working with one at a time. Fill each jar to ¼ inch from the top. Using a plastic spatula, disperse any air bubbles, then clean the rim and threads of the jar before covering with a lid and securing with a screw band. Repeat with the remaining jars.

Process the filled jars in a boiling-water canner for 5 minutes at sea level (see page 16). Let cool, clean the jars, and label before storing.

To serve, these preserves taste good with thick bread and butter.

For green grape & almond conserve, prepare the recipe as above, but add the grated rind of 1 small orange with the grated lemon, and when the conserve has reached setting point, stir in 3 tablespoons slivered almonds.

mixed berry preserves

Makes **about six ½-pint jars**
Preparation time **20 minutes**
Cooking time **40–50 minutes**
(not including canning time)

4 cups **red currants**, stripped
   from stems
juice of **1 lemon**
150 ml (¼ pint) **water**
2⅔ cups **strawberries** (1 lb),
   hulled and halved if large
4 cups **raspberries**
7½ cups **granulated sugar**
1 tablespoon **butter** (optional)

Prepare a boiling-water canner (see pages 16–17).
Sterilize the jars and lids. Set the screw bands aside.

Add the red currants to a large saucepan and
coarsely crush with a vegetable masher. Add the
lemon juice and measured water, cover, and cook
gently for 20–25 minutes, until soft.

Stir in the strawberries and raspberries, then cook
for 5 minutes, until just beginning to soften.

Pour the sugar into the pan and heat gently, stirring
occasionally, until dissolved. Bring to a boil, then boil
rapidly until setting point is reached (20–25 minutes).
Skim with a skimming spoon or stir in butter, if needed.

Ladle into the sterilized jars, working with one at a
time. Fill each jar to ¼ inch from the top. Using a plastic
spatula, disperse any air bubbles, then clean the rim and
threads of the jar before covering with a lid and securing
with a screw band. Repeat with the remaining jars.

Process the filled jars in a boiling-water canner for
5 minutes at sea level (see page 16). Let cool, clean
the jars, and label before storing.

To serve, these preserves make an excellent topping
for individual warm sponge cakes.

For frozen mixed berry preserves, follow the recipe
as above, but use 3 (1-lb) bags frozen mixed berries
instead of the fresh fruit and omit the water.

banana & chocolate jam

Makes **about three ½-pint jars**
Preparation time **20 minutes**
Cooking time **6 minutes**
(not including canning time)

8 **bananas** (about 2 lb),
   peeled and sliced
juice of 1 **lemon**
1 cup **water**
1 (1¾-oz) box **powdered
   pectin**
2½ cups **granulated sugar**
1 tablespoon **butter** (optional)
4 oz **semisweet dark
   chocolate**, broken into pieces

Prepare a boiling-water canner (see pages 16–17) and heat the cleaned jars and lids in simmering water. Set the screw bands aside.

Add the bananas and lemon juice to a medium saucepan and toss together. Add the measured water, then cook gently, uncovered, for 5 minutes, until the bananas are just beginning to soften. Add the pectin and mix until the pectin is completely dissolved.

Bring to a boil, then add the sugar, return to a full rolling boil, and boil rapidly for 1 minute. Skim with a skimming spoon or stir in butter, if needed. Turn off the heat and stir in the chocolate.

Ladle into the warmed jars, working with one at a time. Fill each jar to ¼ inch from the top. Using a plastic spatula, disperse any air bubbles, then clean the rim and threads of the jar before covering with a lid and securing with a screw band. Repeat with the remaining jars.

Process the filled jars in a boiling-water canner for 10 minutes at sea level (see page 16). Let cool, clean the jars, and label before storing.

To serve, this jam can be spread over crepes or waffles and dusted with confectioners' sugar.

For banana & date preserves, follow the recipe as above, but omit the chocolate and add ⅔ cup pitted and chopped dates and 1 teaspoon ground ginger when cooking the bananas.

fruit butters, curds, & pastes

apple, apricot, & elderflower butter

Makes **about six ½-pint jars**
Preparation time **30 minutes**
Cooking time **1 hour**
   25 minutes–1 hour
   30 minutes
(not including canning time)

6 **cooking apples** (about 2 lb),
   quartered, cored, peeled,
   and diced
2 cups diced **dried apricots**
1 **lemon**, finely chopped,
   including pith and peel
2½ cups **water**
about 3 cups **granulated
   sugar**
1 tablespoon **butter** (optional)
3 tablespoons **undiluted
   elderflower syrup (cordial)**

Prepare a boiling-water canner (see pages 16–17) and heat the cleaned jars and lids in simmering water. Set the screw bands aside.

Add the apples, apricots, lemon, and measured water to a medium saucepan. Cover and simmer gently for 1 hour, stirring occasionally, until the fruit is soft.

Puree the fruit, in batches, in a food processor or blender with the cooking water, or press through a strainer. Weigh the puree, then return to the saucepan. For every 1 lb of puree, add 1¼ cups sugar.

Heat gently, stirring occasionally, until the sugar has dissolved. Increase the heat to medium and cook for 25–30 minutes, stirring more frequently toward the end of cooking, until the fruit mixture has darkened to a rich amber, is thick, creamy, and glossy, and drops slowly from a wooden spoon. Skim with a skimming spoon or stir in butter, if needed. Stir in the elderflower syrup.

Ladle into the warmed jars, working with one at a time. Fill each jar to ¼ inch from the top. Using a plastic spatula, disperse any air bubbles, then clean the rim and threads of the jar before covering with a lid and securing with a screw band. Repeat with the remaining jars.

Process the filled jars in a boiling-water canner for 10 minutes at sea level (see page 16). Let cool, clean the jars, and label before storing.

For apple, prune, & vanilla butter, follow the recipe as above, but add 2 cups pitted prunes instead of the apricots and flavor with 2 teaspoons vanilla extract instead of the elderflower syrup.

pear & strawberry butter

Makes **two to three**
  ½-pint jars
Preparation time **25 minutes**
Cooking time **55–60 minutes**
(not including canning time)

4–5 **pears** (about 1½ lb),
  quartered, cored, peeled,
  and sliced
juice of 1 **lemon**
1 quart **strawberries**, hulled
  and sliced (about 4½ cups)
2½ cups **water**
about 3¾ cups **granulated**
  sugar
1 tablespoon **butter** (optional)

Prepare a boiling-water canner (see pages 16–17) and heat the cleaned jars and lids in simmering water. Set the screw bands aside.

Add the pears and lemon juice to a saucepan and toss together, then add the strawberries and measured water. Cover and simmer gently for 30 minutes, stirring occasionally, until the fruit is soft and pulpy.

Puree the fruit, in batches, in a food processor or blender with the cooking water or press through a strainer. Weigh the puree, then return to the saucepan. For every 1 lb of puree, add 1¼ cups sugar.

Heat gently, stirring occasionally, until the sugar has dissolved, then increase the heat to medium and cook for 25–30 minutes, stirring more frequently toward the end of cooking, until the fruit mixture has darkened very slightly, is thick, creamy, and glossy, and drops slowly from a wooden spoon. Skim with a skimming spoon or stir in butter, if needed.

Ladle into the warmed jars, working with one at a time. Fill each jar to ¼ inch from the top. Using a plastic spatula, disperse any air bubbles, then clean the rim and threads of the jar before covering with a lid and securing with a screw band. Repeat with the remaining jars.

Process the filled jars in a boiling-water canner for 10 minutes at sea level (see page 16). Let cool, clean the jars, and label before storing.

For pear & plum butter, follow the recipe as above, but replace the strawberries with 10 pitted plums (about 1½ lb).

cranberry & cinnamon butter

Makes **about 12 ½-pint jars**
Preparation time **25 minutes**
Cooking time **1 hour–**
  1 hour 10 minutes
(not including canning time)

10 cups **cranberries,** fresh or
  frozen (no need to defrost)
4¼ cups **water**
rind of 2 **oranges**
about 7½ cups
  granulated sugar
2 teaspoons **ground**
  cinnamon
1 tablespoon **butter** (optional)

Prepare a boiling-water canner (see pages 16–17) and heat the cleaned jars and lids in simmering water. Set the screw bands aside.

Add the cranberries to a saucepan with the measured water, add the orange rind, and bring to a boil. Cover and simmer gently for 30 minutes, stirring occasionally and mashing the fruit with a wooden spoon, until it is soft. Let the cranberries cool slightly. Puree, in small batches, in a food processor or blender or press through a strainer. Weigh the puree and return to the rinsed saucepan. For every 1 lb of puree, add a scant 2 cups sugar, and add the ground cinnamon.

Heat gently, stirring occasionally, until the sugar dissolves. Increase the heat to medium and cook for 30–40 minutes, stirring more often toward the end of cooking, until the mixture has reduced by almost half, is darker, thick, and glossy, and drops slowly from a wooden spoon. Skim with a skimming spoon or stir in butter, if needed.

Ladle into the warmed jars, working with one at a time. Fill each jar to ¼ inch from the top. Using a plastic spatula, disperse any air bubbles, then clean the rim and threads of the jar before covering with a lid and securing with a screw band. Repeat with the remaining jars.

Process the filled jars in a boiling-water canner for 10 minutes at sea level (see page 16). Let cool, clean the jars, and label before storing.

For cranberry & pear butter, follow the recipe as above, but use 7 cups cranberries with 2 peeled, cored, and diced pears, replace ½ cup water with ½ cup juice from the oranges, and omit the cinnamon.

spiced apple butter

Makes **about three to four**
  ½-pint jars
Preparation time **20 minutes**
Cooking time **1½ hours**
(not including canning time)

7–8 **cooking apples** (about
  2½ lb), coarsely chopped
1 **cinnamon stick**
1 teaspoon **freshly grated
  nutmeg**
1 **lemon**, chopped
2½ cups **water**
about 3¼ cups **granulated
  sugar**

Prepare a boiling-water canner (see pages 16–17).
Sterilize the jars and lids. Set the screw bands aside.

Add the apples, spices, chopped lemon, and measured
water to a saucepan. Bring to a boil, then reduce the
heat and simmer, covered, for 1 hour, or until the fruit
is reduced to a pulp.

Puree the fruit, in small batches, in a food processor or
blender. Press the mixture through a fine strainer, then
weigh the puree and put it into a clean pan. For every
1 lb of puree, add 2 cups sugar and cook over low heat,
stirring continuously, until the sugar has completely
dissolved. Increase the heat to medium, then cook for
about 30 minutes, stirring frequently, until the mixture is
reduced by half, is thick and glossy, and falls slowly from
a wooden spoon.

Ladle into the sterilized jars, working with one at a
time. Fill each jar to ¼ inch from the top. Using a plastic
spatula, disperse any air bubbles, then clean the rim and
threads of the jar before covering with a lid and securing
with a screw band. Repeat with the remaining jars.

To serve, enjoy this preserve with cheese and biscuits.

Process the filled jars in a boiling-water canner for
5 minutes at sea level (see page 16). Let cool, clean
the jars, and label before storing.

For apple & ginger wine butter, follow the recipe as
above, but add 1 coarsely chopped lemon with the apples
and substitute ½ cup water for ½ cup ginger wine.

spiced pumpkin butter

Makes **about three ½-pint jars**
Preparation time **30 minutes**
Cooking time **30 minutes**
(not including canning time)

10 cups peeled, seeded,
   and cubed **pie pumpkin**
   (¾-inch pieces)
2 cups **granulated sugar**
1 teaspoon **ground ginger**
1 teaspoon **ground allspice**
6 pieces **preserved ginger**
   in syrup, finely chopped
1 tablespoon **butter** (optional)

Prepare a boiling-water canner (see pages 16–17) and heat the cleaned jars and lids in simmering water. Set the screw bands aside.

Steam the pumpkin for about 15 minutes, until tender. Let cool slightly, then puree in a blender or food processor or press through a strainer until smooth. Weigh the puree, then pour into a saucepan. For every 1 lb of puree, add 1¼ cups sugar.

Stir in the spices and ginger, then heat gently, stirring occasionally, until the sugar has dissolved. Increase the heat to medium and cook for about 15 minutes, stirring more frequently toward the end of cooking, until the fruit mixture has darkened slightly, is thick, creamy, and glossy, and drops slowly from a wooden spoon. Skim with a skimming spoon or stir in butter, if needed.

Ladle into the warmed jars, working with one at a time. Fill each jar to ¼ inch from the top. Using a plastic spatula, disperse any air bubbles, then clean the rim and threads of the jar before covering with a lid and securing with a screw band. Repeat with the remaining jars.

Process the filled jars in a boiling-water canner for 10 minutes at sea level (see page 16). Let cool, clean the jars, and label before storing.

To serve, this butter can be used in tiny lattice-topped tarts to make baby pumpkin pies.

For pumpkin & brown sugar butter, follow the recipe as above, but replace the granulated sugar with light brown sugar. Stir in the ground spices but omit the chopped ginger.

st. clement's curd

Makes **about two ½-pint jars**
Preparation time **25 minutes**
Cooking time **40–50 minutes**

1 stick **butter**, diced
2 cups **superfine sugar**
grated rind and juice of
    2 **lemons**
grated rind and juice of
    1 **orange**
grated rind and juice of **1 lime**
4 **eggs**, beaten

Sterilize the jars and lids.

Heat the butter in a large bowl set over a saucepan of simmering water until melted.

Pour the sugar into the melted butter, then add the grated fruit rinds. Strain in the fruit juices, discarding any seeds, then strain in the beaten eggs and mix together. Cook for 40–50 minutes, stirring occasionally, until the sugar has dissolved and the mixture has thickened.

Ladle into sterilized, dry jars, let cool, cover, and store in the refrigerator for up to 1 week.

For traditional lemon curd, follow the recipe as above, but use the grated rind and juice of 3 large lemons in place of the lemons, orange, and lime.

apple & ginger curd

Makes **about three** ½-**pint jars**
Preparation time **25 minutes**
Cooking time **55–65 minutes**

4–5 **cooking apples**
　(about 1 ½ lb), quartered,
　cored, peeled, and diced
⅓ cup **ginger wine**
grated rind and juice of
　1 **lemon**
1 stick **butter**, diced
2 cups **superfine sugar**
3 **eggs**, beaten
4 pieces **preserved ginger in**
　syrup, finely chopped

Sterilize the jars and lids.

Add the apples, ginger wine, and lemon rind and juice to a saucepan, then cover and cook gently for about 15 minutes, stirring occasionally, until the apples are soft. Let cool for 10–15 minutes.

Puree the apple mixture in a food processor or blender or press through a strainer. Place the butter in a large bowl set over a saucepan of simmering water and warm until just melted.

Add the sugar and apple puree to the bowl, then strain in the eggs and cook over medium heat for 40–50 minutes, stirring frequently until the sugar has dissolved and the eggs have thickened the mixture (be careful not to have the heat too high or the eggs will curdle). Stir in the chopped ginger.

Ladle into sterilized, dry jars, let cool, cover, and store in the refrigerator for up to 1 week.

For spiced apple curd, follow the recipe as above, but add 4 cloves and a 2-inch cinnamon stick with the lemon, omit the chopped ginger, and remove the spices before pureeing.

raspberry & red grapefruit curd

Makes **about two ½-pint jars**
Preparation time **20 minutes**
Cooking time **40–50 minutes**

1½ cups **raspberries**
juice of 1 **red grapefruit**
1 stick **butter**, diced
2 cups **superfine sugar**
4 **eggs**, beaten
few drops **red food coloring**
  (optional)

Sterilize the jars and lids.

Puree the raspberries with the grapefruit juice in a food processor or blender until smooth, then press through a strainer and discard the raspberry seeds.

Heat the butter in a large bowl set over a saucepan of simmering water until melted. Stir in the sugar and raspberry puree, then strain in the eggs and mix together. Cook for 40–50 minutes, stirring occasionally, until the sugar has dissolved and mixture has thickened. Stir in a few drops of food coloring, if desired.

Ladle into sterilized, dry jars, let cool, cover, and store in the refrigerator for up to 1 week.

To serve, this curd can be teamed with shortbread cookies, whipped cream, and whole raspberries for a dainty dessert.

For raspberry & lemon curd, follow the recipe as above, but omit the grapefruit juice and add the grated rind and juice of 2 lemons, adding the grated rind when mixing the fruit puree into the melted butter and sugar mix.

lime & passion fruit curd

Makes **about two ½-pint jars**
Preparation time **15 minutes**
Cooking time **30–40 minutes**

1¼ cups **superfine sugar**
finely grated rind and juice
  of 4 **limes**
1 stick **unsalted butter**,
  cut into pieces
4 **eggs**, beaten
3 **passion fruit**

Sterilize the jars and lids.

Heat the sugar and lime rind in a bowl set over
a saucepan of simmering water, pressing the rind
against the side of the bowl, using a wooden spoon,
to release the oils.

Strain the lime juice into the bowl and add the butter.
Heat, stirring occasionally, until the butter has melted.
Strain the eggs into the mixture and mix together.
Continue heating gently for 20–30 minutes, stirring
occasionally, until the mixture is very thick. Remove
the bowl from the heat.

Halve the passion fruit, then scoop the seeds into
the lime curd. Mix together gently.

Ladle into sterilized, dry jars, let cool, cover, and store
in the refrigerator for up to 1 week.

For lime & coconut curd, stir ¼ cup unsweetened
dry coconut into the curd mixture after adding the
strained eggs.

gooseberry curd

Makes **about two ½-pint jars**
Preparation time **25 minutes**
Cooking time **55–60 minutes**

1½ cups **gooseberries**,
   trimmed
grated rind and juice of
   1 **lemon**
¼ cup **water**
1 stick **butter**
2 cups **superfine sugar**
4 **eggs**, beaten
few drops **green food
   coloring** (optional)

Sterilize the jars and lids.

Add the gooseberries, lemon rind and juice, and measured water to a medium saucepan, cover, and cook gently for 15 minutes, until the gooseberries are soft. Let cool slightly, then puree in a food processor or blender and press through a strainer to remove the seeds.

Heat the butter in a large bowl set over a saucepan of simmering water until melted. Stir in the sugar and gooseberry puree, then strain in the eggs, and mix together. Cook for 40–50 minutes, stirring occasionally, until the sugar has dissolved and the mixture has thickened. Stir in a few drops of food coloring, if desired.

Ladle into sterilized, dry jars, let cool, cover, and store in the refrigerator for up to 1 week.

To serve, this curd tastes good with warmed croissants.

For gooseberry & elderflower curd, stir 3 tablespoons undiluted elderflower syrup (cordial) into the bowl when adding the eggs. Continue as above.

pear & red wine paste

Makes **about two ½-pint jars**
Preparation time **30 minutes**
Cooking time **1¼–1½ hours**

9 **pears** (about 3 lb),
    quartered, cored, peeled,
    and sliced
1 teaspoon **cloves**, roughly
    crushed
1¼ cups **red wine**
1¼ cups **water**
about 7½ cups **granulated
    sugar**
1 tablespoon **butter**, optional

Sterilize the jars and lids.

Add the pears and crushed cloves to a saucepan. Pour over the wine and measured water to just cover the bottom of the pan, then bring to a boil. Cover and cook gently for 30 minutes, stirring occasionally and breaking up the pears with a wooden spoon or vegetable masher, until very soft.

Let cool slightly, then puree in small batches in a food processor or blender, or press through a strainer.

Weigh the puree, then pour back into the rinsed saucepan. For every 1 lb of puree, add scant 2 cups sugar. Heat gently, stirring occasionally, until the sugar has dissolved.

Cook over medium heat for 45–60 minutes, stirring more frequently toward the end of cooking, until the mixture has darkened slightly and is so thick that the wooden spoon leaves a line across the bottom of the pan when drawn through the mixture. Skim with a skimming spoon or stir in the butter, if needed.

Ladle into sterilized, dry jars, let cool, cover, and store in the refrigerator for up to 1 week before using. It will keep for up to 1 year.

To serve, this makes a good accompaniment for cheese, crackers, and grapes.

For plum & clove paste, use 3 lb plums—count them—and add to the saucepan with the cloves and 2½ cups water. Cook as above, then remove the pits, making sure to count them to double-check that you have them all, before pureeing and continuing as above.

quince paste

Makes **about four ½-pint wide-neck jars**
Preparation time **45 minutes**
Cooking time **1¾–2 hours**

4 lb **quinces**, rubbed off, rinsed, and cut into 1-inch cubes
8¾ cups **water**
7½–8¾ cups **granulated sugar**
a little **sunflower oil**
1 tablespoon **butter** (optional)

Sterilize the jars and lids.

Add the quinces to a large pan and pour over the measured water. Cover and bring to a boil, then reduce the heat and simmer for 1 hour, until very soft.

Puree the quinces and their liquid, in batches, in a food processor or blender, then press through a strainer into a large bowl. Discard the seeds, skin, and cores. Weigh the puree. Wash and dry the pan and brush with sunflower oil. Pour the puree back into the pan, add 2½ cups sugar for every 1 lb puree, and cook over low heat, stirring occasionally, until the sugar has dissolved.

Cook, uncovered, over medium heat for 45–60 minutes, stirring more frequently toward the end of cooking, until the mixture makes large bubbles, has darkened slightly, and is so thick that the wooden spoon leaves a line across the bottom of the pan when drawn through the mixture. Skim with a skimming spoon or stir in the butter, if needed.

Ladle quickly into sterilized, warm, wide-neck jars with tight-fitting lids (square, if possible), the insides of which have been lightly brushed with sunflower oil, filling to the top. Cover, label, and let cool.

To serve, loosen the quince cheese with a blunt knife, turn out, and slice. Serve with bread and cheese.

For blackberry & apple paste, quarter, core, and peel 9 cooking apples (about 3 lb), and cook with 3½ cups blackberries and 2½ cups water for 30 minutes, until soft. Puree, then weigh and add to the saucepan with 2 cups sugar for every 1 lb puree. Continue as above.

jellies

plum & crushed peppercorn jelly

Makes **about seven**
  ½-pint jars
Preparation time **25 minutes,**
  plus straining
Cooking time **40–50 minutes**
(not including canning time)

2 quarts **plums** (about 4 lb),
  left whole
5 cups **water**
about 6¼ cups **granulated**
  sugar
2 teaspoons **multicolored**
  peppercorns, coarsely
  crushed
2 teaspoons **pink**
  peppercorns, either dried or
  in brine, coarsely crushed
1 tablespoon **butter** (optional)

Prepare a boiling-water canner (see pages 16–17).
Sterilize the jars and lids. Set the screw bands aside.

Add the plums and measured water to a large
saucepan. Bring to a boil, cover, and cook gently
for 30 minutes, stirring and mashing occasionally
with a fork, until soft.

Let cool slightly, pour into a scalded jelly bag suspended
over a large bowl, and let drip for several hours.

Measure the clear liquid and pour back into the rinsed
saucepan. Add 2½ cups sugar for every 2½ cups
liquid. Add the peppercorns and heat gently, stirring
occasionally, until the sugar has dissolved.

Bring to a boil, then boil rapidly until setting point is
reached (10–20 minutes). Skim with a skimming spoon
or stir in butter, if needed. Allow to stand for 5 minutes
so that the peppercorns don't float to the surface.

Ladle into the sterilized jars, working with one at a time.
Fill each jar to ¼ inch from the top. Clean the rim and
threads of the jar before covering with a lid and securing
with a screw band. Repeat with the remaining jars.

Process the filled jars in a boiling-water canner for
5 minutes at sea level (see page 16). Let cool, clean
the jars, and label before storing.

To serve, this jelly works well with roasted lamb and
roasted potatoes.

For plum & star anise jelly, add 7 small star anise
instead of the peppercorns and make sure to include
1 per jar when canning.

gooseberry & rosemary jelly

Makes **about four ½-pint jars**
Preparation time **25 minutes,
  plus straining**
Cooking time **30–45 minutes**
(not including canning time)

3¾ cups **gooseberries**
  (no need to trim)
4¼ cups **water**
4–5 stems **fresh rosemary**
about 4⅓ cups **granulated
  sugar**
1 tablespoon **butter** (optional)

Prepare a boiling-water canner (see pages 16–17). Sterilize the jars and lids. Set the screw bands aside.

Add the gooseberries, measured water, and rosemary to a medium saucepan. Bring to a boil, then cover and simmer gently for 20–30 minutes, stirring and mashing the fruit occasionally with a fork, until soft.

Let cool slightly, pour into a scalded jelly bag suspended over a large bowl, and let drip for several hours.

Measure the clear liquid and pour back into the rinsed saucepan. Add 2½ cups sugar for every 2½ cups liquid, then pour into the saucepan. Heat gently, stirring occasionally, until the sugar has dissolved.

Bring to a boil, then boil rapidly until setting point is reached (10–15 minutes). Skim with a skimming spoon or stir in butter, if needed.

Ladle into the sterilized jars, working with one at a time. Fill each jar to ¼ inch from the top. Clean the rim and threads of the jar before covering with a lid and securing with a screw band. Repeat with the remaining jars.

Process the filled jars in a boiling-water canner for 5 minutes at sea level (see page 16). Let cool, clean the jars, and label before storing.

To serve, try this jelly with broiled herrings and salad.

For sour apple & rosemary jelly, cook 9 cooking apples (about 3 lb), coarsely chopped (no need to peel or core first), with 3 cups water and ⅔ cup white wine vinegar. Add rosemary and cook as above.

windfall apple & cider jelly

Makes **about four 1-pint jars**
Preparation time **25 minutes,
   plus straining**
Cooking time **45–55 minutes**
(not including canning time)

15 **windfall apples** (about
   5 lb), bruised areas cut off
2 cups **hard dry cider**
3¾ cups **water**
rind of 1 **lemon**
about 5 cups **granulated
   sugar**
1 tablespoon **butter** (optional)

Prepare a boiling-water canner (see pages 16–17).
Sterilize the jars and lids. Set the screw bands aside.

Wash and coarsely chop the apples, without peeling
or coring first. Add to a large saucepan with the cider,
measured water, and lemon rind. Bring to a boil, then
cover and simmer gently for 30 minutes, stirring and
mashing the fruit occasionally with a fork, until soft.

Let cool slightly, pour into a scalded jelly bag suspended
over a large bowl, and let drip for several hours.

Measure the clear liquid and pour back into the rinsed
saucepan. Add 2½ cups sugar for every 2½ cups
liquid. Heat gently, stirring occasionally, until the sugar
has dissolved.

Bring to a boil, then boil rapidly until setting point is
reached (15–25 minutes). Skim with a skimming spoon
or stir in butter, if needed.

Ladle into the sterilized jars, working with one at a time.
Fill each jar to ¼ inch from the top. Clean the rim and
threads of the jar before covering with a lid and securing
with a screw band. Repeat with the remaining jars.

Process the filled jars in a boiling-water canner for
5 minutes at sea level (see page 16). Let cool, clean
the jars, and label before storing.

For windfall apple & ginger jelly, omit the cider and
add 2 cups extra water. Cook, then drip as above. Add a
2-inch piece of ginger root, peeled and finely chopped,
when adding the sugar. Continue as above.

bloody mary jelly

Makes **about four ½-pint jars**
Preparation time **30 minutes,**
  plus straining
Cooking time **1 hour**
  20 minutes–1 hour
  30 minutes
(not including canning time)

2 **red onions**, coarsely
  chopped
3 **celery sticks**, coarsely
  chopped
8 **tomatoes** (about 2 lb),
  coarsely chopped (not
  skinned or seeded)
3 **cooking apples**, coarsely
  chopped (not peeled or
  cored)
2½ cups **water**
¾ cup plus 2 tablespoons
  red wine vinegar
about 6¼ cups **granulated
  sugar**
1 tablespoon **tomato paste**
juice of 2 **lemons**
1 tablespoon **butter**, optional
⅓ cup drained, diced
  sun-dried tomatoes in oil
¼ cup **vodka** (optional)

Prepare a boiling-water canner (see pages 16–17).
Sterilize the jars and lids. Set the screw bands aside.

Add the onions, celery, tomatoes, and apples to a
saucepan. Pour in the measured water and vinegar,
then bring to a boil. Reduce the heat, cover, and simmer
gently for 1 hour, stirring and mashing occasionally with
a fork, until the tomatoes and apples are pulpy. Let cool
slightly, pour into a scalded jelly bag suspended over a
large bowl, and let drip for several hours.

Measure the clear liquid and pour back into the rinsed
saucepan. Add 2½ cups sugar for every 2½ cups liquid.
Add the tomato paste and lemon juice and heat gently,
stirring occasionally, until the sugar has dissolved.

Bring to a boil, then boil rapidly until setting point is
reached (20–30 minutes). Skim with a skimming spoon
or stir in butter, if needed. Stir in the sun-dried tomatoes
and vodka, if desired, and let stand for 15 minutes so
that the tomatoes don't rise in the jelly when canned.

Ladle into the sterilized jars, working with one at a time.
Fill each jar to ¼ inch from the top. Clean the rim and
threads of the jar before covering with a lid and securing
with a screw band. Repeat with the remaining jars.

Process the filled jars in a boiling-water canner for
5 minutes at sea level (see page 16). Let cool, clean
the jars, and label before storing.

To serve, this jelly goes well with cold meats, such as
salami and prosciutto, olives, and sun-dried tomatoes.

For chile tomato jelly, stir in 1 teaspoon dried red
pepper flakes with the tomato puree.

bitter lime & pernod jelly

Makes **about three ½-pint jars**
Preparation time **25 minutes,**
  plus straining
Cooking time **1 hour**
  5 minutes–1 hour
  10 minutes
(not including canning time)

6 large **limes**, coarsely
  chopped
3 **pears**, coarsely chopped
  (no need to peel and core)
5 cups **water**
about 3¾ cups **granulated**
  sugar
⅓ cup **Pernod**
1 tablespoon **butter** (optional)

Prepare a boiling-water canner (see pages 16–17).
Sterilize the jars and lids. Set the screw bands aside.

Add the limes, pears, and measured water to a medium
saucepan, bring to a boil, cover, and cook gently for
1 hour, stirring and mashing the fruit occasionally
with a fork, until soft.

Let cool slightly, pour into a scalded jelly bag suspended
over a large bowl, and let drip for several hours.

Measure the clear liquid and pour back into the rinsed
saucepan. Add 2½ cups sugar for every 2½ cups liquid.
Add the Pernod and cook gently, stirring occasionally,
until the sugar has dissolved.

Bring to a boil, then boil rapidly until setting point is
reached (5–10 minutes). Skim with a skimming spoon
or stir in butter, if needed.

Ladle into the sterilized jars, working with one at a time.
Fill each jar to ¼ inch from the top. Clean the rim and
threads of the jar before covering with a lid and securing
with a screw band. Repeat with the remaining jars.

Process the filled jars in a boiling-water canner for
5 minutes at sea level (see page 16). Let cool, clean
the jars, and label before storing.

To serve, try spreading baguette slices with cream cheese,
then top with smoked salmon, jelly, and watercress.

For bitter lemon & lime jelly, replace the limes with
a mixture of lemons and limes, then continue as above,
omitting the Pernod.

rosehip & apple jelly

Makes **about four ½-pint jars**
Preparation time **30 minutes,
  plus straining**
Cooking time **55 minutes–
  1 ¼ hours**
(not including canning time)

12 oz ripe **red rosehips**,
  left whole
6 **cooking apples** (about 2 lb),
  coarsely chopped (no need
  to peel or core)
4 ¼ cups **water**
about 4 ⅓ cups **granulated
  sugar**
juice of **1 lemon**
1 tablespoon **butter** (optional)

Prepare a boiling-water canner (see pages 16–17).
Sterilize the jars and lids. Set the screw bands aside.

Add the rosehips and apples to a saucepan with the
measured water. Bring to a boil, then cover and simmer
gently for 45–60 minutes, stirring and mashing the fruit
occasionally with a fork, until soft.

Let cool slightly, pour into a scalded jelly bag suspended
over a large bowl, and let drip for several hours.

Measure the clear liquid and pour back into the rinsed
saucepan. Add 2 ½ cups sugar for every 2 ½ cups
liquid. Add the lemon juice and heat gently, stirring
occasionally, until the sugar has dissolved.

Bring to a boil, then boil rapidly until setting point is
reached (10–15 minutes). Skim with a skimming spoon
or stir in butter, if needed.

Ladle into the sterilized jars, working with one at a time.
Fill each jar to ¼ inch from the top. Clean the rim and
threads of the jar before covering with a lid and securing
with a screw band. Repeat with the remaining jars.

Process the filled jars in a boiling-water canner for
5 minutes at sea level (see page 16). Let cool, clean
the jars, and label before storing.

For elderberry & apple jelly, make up the jelly with
4 ½ cups elderberries, stripped from their stems,
and 4–5 cooking apples (about 1 ½ lb), coarsely chopped
but not peeled or cored, and cook in 3 ¾ cups water for
40 minutes, until the fruit is soft. Continue as above.

minted blackberry & apple jelly

Makes **about six ½-pint jars**
Preparation time **25 minutes,
   plus straining**
Cooking time **40 minutes–
   1 hour**
(not including canning time)

12 **cooking apples**
   (about 4 lb)**,** coarsely
   chopped (no need
   to peel or core)
3½ cups **blackberries**
5 cups **water**
7½ cups g**ranulated sugar**
1 tablespoon **butter** (optional)
⅓ cup finely chopped
   fresh **mint**

Prepare a boiling-water canner (see pages 16–17).
Sterilize the jars and lids. Set the screw bands aside.

Add the apples, blackberries, and measured water
to a large saucepan, bring to a boil, then cover and cook
gently for 30–40 minutes, stirring and mashing the fruit
occasionally with a fork, until soft.

Let cool slightly, pour into a scalded jelly bag suspended
over a large bowl, and let drip for several hours.

Measure the clear liquid and pour back into the
rinsed saucepan. Add 2½ cups sugar for every 2½ cups
liquid. Heat gently, stirring occasionally, until the sugar
has dissolved. Bring to a boil, then boil rapidly until
setting point is reached (10–20 minutes). Skim with a
draining spoon or stir in butter, if needed. Let cool for
5–10 minutes, then stir in the mint.

Ladle into the sterilized jars, working with one at a time.
Fill each jar to ¼ inch from the top. Clean the rim and
threads of the jar before covering with a lid and securing
with a screw band. Repeat with the remaining jars.

Process the filled jars in a boiling-water canner for
5 minutes at sea level (see page 16). Let cool, clean
the jars, and label before storing.

To serve, this jelly is a great accompaniment for
pancakes with butter.

For quince, apple, & cinnamon jelly, coarsely chop
7–8 cooking apples (about 2½ lb) and 2½ lb quinces,
then add to the saucepan with a 3-inch cinnamon stick,
broken in half, and 5 cups water. Cover and cook gently,
as above.

106

red currant & lavender jelly

Makes **about six ½-pint jars**
Preparation time **25 minutes,**
   plus straining
Cooking time **30–40 minutes**
(not including canning time)

12 cups **red currants**
   (about 3 lb)
4¼ cups **water**
about 5 cups **granulated**
   sugar
1 tablespoon **butter** (optional)
8–10 **dried lavender heads**

Prepare a boiling-water canner (see pages 16–17). Sterilize the jars and lids. Set the screw bands aside.

Strip the red currants from their stems with a fork and add to a saucepan with the measured water. Bring to a boil, cover, and simmer gently for 20 minutes, stirring and mashing occasionally with a fork, until soft.

Let cool slightly, pour into a scalded jelly bag suspended over a large bowl, and let drip for several hours.

Measure the liquid and pour back into the rinsed saucepan. Add 2½ cups sugar for every 2½ cups liquid. Heat gently, stirring occasionally, until the sugar has dissolved.

Bring to a boil, then boil rapidly until setting point is reached (10–20 minutes). Skim with a skimming spoon or stir in butter, if needed. Stir in the lavender and let cool for 5–10 minutes.

Ladle into the sterilized jars, working with one at a time. Fill each jar to ¼ inch from the top. Clean the rim and threads of the jar before covering with a lid and securing with a screw band. Repeat with the remaining jars.

Process the filled jars in a boiling-water canner for 5 minutes at sea level (see page 16). Let cool, clean the jars, and label before storing.

To serve, spoon onto a cream-topped pavlova with extra strawberries.

For red currant & orange jelly, reduce the amount of water to 3¾ cups when cooking the red currants, then add the juice of 2 oranges when measuring out the juice at the end. Omit the lavender flowers.

strawberry & rhubarb jelly

Makes **about eight ½-pint jars**
Preparation time **25 minutes,**
  plus straining
Cooking time **50–60 minutes**
(not including canning time)

1½ quarts **strawberries,**
  halved if large
1 lb **rhubarb,** trimmed and
  thickly sliced
4¼ cups **water**
about 4⅓ cups **granulated**
  sugar
juice of 2 **lemons**
1 tablespoon **butter** (optional)

Prepare a boiling-water canner (see pages 16–17). Sterilize the jars and lids. Set the screw bands aside.

Add the strawberries and rhubarb to a large saucepan, pour over the measured water to just cover the fruit, and bring to a boil. Cover and simmer gently for 30 minutes, stirring and mashing occasionally with a fork, until soft.

Let cool slightly, pour into a scalded jelly bag suspended over a large bowl, and let drip for several hours.

Measure the clear liquid and pour back into the rinsed saucepan. Add 2½ cups sugar for every 2½ cups liquid. Add the lemon juice, heat gently, stirring occasionally, until the sugar has dissolved. Bring to a boil, then boil rapidly until setting point is reached (20–30 minutes). Skim with a skimming spoon or stir in butter, if needed.

Ladle into the sterilized jars, working with one at a time. Fill each jar to ¼ inch from the top. Clean the rim and threads of the jar before covering with a lid and securing with a screw band. Repeat with the remaining jars.

Process the filled jars in a boiling-water canner for 5 minutes at sea level (see page 16). Let cool, clean the jars, and label before storing.

To serve, this jelly makes a great filling for a jelly roll.

For mulberry & apple jelly, cook 3 coarsely chopped cooking apples in 1¼ cups water in a covered saucepan for 10 minutes, until just beginning to soften. Add 6½ cups mulberries and cook for 20 minutes, stirring and crushing occasionally, until soft. Strain and continue as above.

grape & port jelly

Makes **about three to four
½-pint jars**
Preparation time **10 minutes,
plus straining**
Cooking time **1 hour
10 minutes–1 hour
15 minutes**
(not including canning time)

2 lb **red grapes with stems**,
halved
3 **lemons**, halved
7¾ cups **water**
about 3¾ cups **granulated
sugar**
⅔ cup **port**
1 tablespoon **butter** (optional)

Prepare a boiling-water canner (see pages 16–17).
Sterilize the jars and lids. Set the screw bands aside.

Add the grapes and their stems to a large saucepan.
Squeeze and reserve the juice from the lemons. Chop
the lemon shells and add to the pan with the measured
water. Bring to a boil, reduce the heat, and cover the
pan. Simmer for 1 hour.

Let cool slightly, pour into a scalded jelly bag suspended
over a large bowl, and let drip for several hours.

Measure the clear liquid and pour back into the rinsed
saucepan. Add 2½ cups sugar for every 2½ cups liquid.
Pour in the port and reserved lemon juice and cook over
low heat, stirring continuously, until the sugar has
dissolved. Bring to a boil, then boil rapidly until setting
point is reached (10–15 minutes). Skim with a
skimming spoon or stir in butter, if needed.

Ladle into the sterilized jars, working with one at a time.
Fill each jar to ¼ inch from the top. Clean the rim and
threads of the jar before covering with a lid and securing
with a screw band. Repeat with the remaining jars.

Process the filled jars in a boiling-water canner for
5 minutes at sea level (see page 16). Let cool, clean
the jars, and label before storing.

To serve, drizzle the jelly over vanilla ice cream.

For crab apple jelly, coarsely chop 4 lb crab apples
and add to a saucepan with 5 cups water, the juice of
2 lemons, and 4 cloves. Cover and simmer for 1½ hours,
strain, then add 2 cups granulated sugar for every
2½ cups juice. Continue as above.

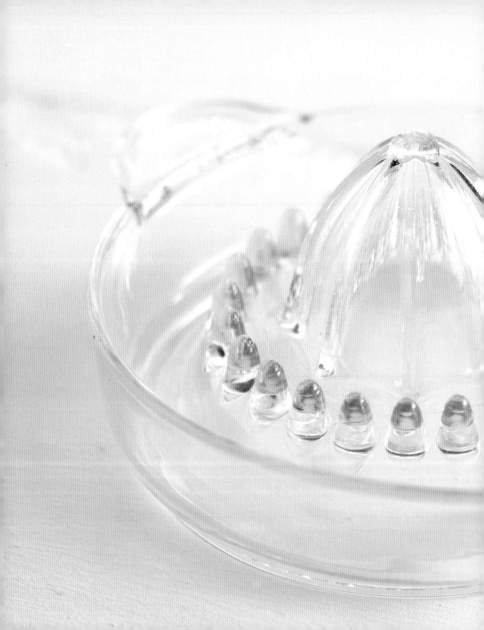

marmalades

dark oxford marmalade

Makes **about five to six**
½-pint jars
Preparation time **30 minutes**
Cooking time **1 hour**
40 minutes–1 hour
50 minutes
(not including canning time)

6 Seville or regular **oranges**
(about 2 lb)
7¾ cups **water**
juice of 1 **lemon**
8¾ cups **granulated sugar**
1 cup **dark brown sugar**
1 tablespoon **butter** (optional)

Prepare a boiling-water canner (see pages 16–17). Sterilize the jars and lids. Set the screw bands aside.

Cut each orange into 6 wedges, then thinly slice. Tie the orange seeds in a square of cheesecloth. Add the oranges and seeds to a large saucepan, pour in the measured water, and add the lemon juice. Bring slowly to a boil, then simmer gently, uncovered, for about 1½ hours, until reduced by almost half.

Add the sugar and heat gently, stirring occasionally, until dissolved. Bring to a boil, then boil rapidly until setting point is reached (10–20 minutes).

Lift out the cheesecloth bag, squeezing well. Skim with a draining spoon or stir in butter, if needed.

Ladle into the sterilized jars, working with one at a time. Fill each jar to ¼ inch from the top. Clean the rim and threads of the jar before covering with a lid and securing with a screw band. Repeat with the remaining jars.

Process the filled jars in a boiling-water canner for 5 minutes at sea level (see page 16). Let cool, clean the jars, and label before storing.

To serve, this marmalade goes wonderfully with sliced walnut bread.

For golden Oxford marmalade, follow the recipe as above, but omit the dark brown sugar and increase the granulated sugar to 10 cups.

apple & orange marmalade

Makes **about 10 ½-pint jars**
Preparation time **30 minutes**
Cooking time **1 hour**
50 minutes–2½ hours

4–5 **oranges** (about 1½ lb),
chopped and seeds tied in a
square of cheesecloth with
the lemon seeds
2 **lemons**, chopped and
seeds tied in a square of
cheesecloth with the orange
seeds
5–6½ cups **water**
6 **apples** (about 2 lb), peeled,
quartered, and cored
8¾ cups **granulated sugar**
1 tablespoon **butter**

Prepare a boiling-water canner (see pages 16–17).
Sterilize the jars and lids. Set the screw bands aside.

Add the oranges, lemons, and cheesecloth bag of
seeds to the pan. Pour in 4¼ cups water, bring to a boil,
cover, and simmer for 1½–2 hours. Stir occasionally,
making sure the fruit doesn't boil dry. Add a little extra
water, if needed. Meanwhile, add the apples to another
saucepan with ⅔ cup water. Cover and cook gently for
20 minutes, stirring occasionally, until soft.

Let the fruits cool. Lift out the cheesecloth bag, squeezing
well. Blend the fruits together, in small batches, in a food
processor or blender, adding the remaining water as
needed to aid blending. Pour back into a saucepan, add
the sugar, then heat gently, stirring occasionally, until
the sugar has dissolved. Bring to a boil, then boil rapidly
until setting point is reached (20–30 minutes). Skim
with a draining spoon or stir in butter, if needed.

Ladle into the sterilized jars, working with one at a time.
Fill each jar to ¼ inch from the top. Clean the rim and
threads of the jar before covering with a lid and securing
with a screw band. Repeat with the remaining jars.

Process the filled jars in a boiling-water canner for
5 minutes at sea level (see page 16). Let cool, clean
the jars, and label before storing.

To serve, try it with hot, buttered English muffins.

For chunky fig, almond, & orange marmalade, replace
the apples with 2¾ cups dried chopped figs in 1¼ cups
water. Puree the cooked figs together with the citrus fruit,
then add to the saucepan with ½ cup coarsely chopped
blanched almonds and the sugar, and continue as above.

apricot, orange, & ginger marmalade

Makes **about 10 ½-pint jars**
Preparation time **25 minutes,
  plus soaking**
Cooking time **1 hour–1 hour
  5 minutes**
(not including canning time)

3 **oranges** (about 1 lb)
1 **lemon**
2 cups diced **dried apricots**
2-inch **piece ginger root,**
  peeled and finely chopped
5 cups **water**
7½ cups **granulated sugar**
1 tablespoon **butter** (optional)

Prepare a boiling-water canner (see pages 16–17). Sterilize the jars and lids. Set the screw bands aside.

Halve the oranges and lemon and squeeze out the juice into a bowl. Scrape out the pith and seeds and tie in a cheesecloth bag. Cut the fruit shells into thin slices. Add the apricots and ginger to the fruit juice and mix in the measured water, then add the cheesecloth bag. Cover the bowl and let soak overnight in a cool place.

Pour the fruit mixture into a saucepan, cover, and cook gently for 45 minutes, until tender. Add the sugar and heat gently, stirring occasionally, until dissolved.

Bring to a boil, then boil rapidly until setting point is reached (15–20 minutes). Lift out the cheesecloth bag, squeezing well. Skim with a draining spoon or add the butter, if needed. Let cool for 10 minutes.

Ladle into the sterilized jars, working with one at a time. Fill each jar to ¼ inch from the top. Clean the rim and threads of the jar before covering with a lid and securing with a screw band. Repeat with the remaining jars.

Process the filled jars in a boiling-water canner for 5 minutes at sea level (see page 16). Let cool, clean the jars, and label before storing.

To serve, this marmalade makes a good topping for a ginger cake.

For apricot, orange, & cardamom marmalade,
follow the recipe as above, but omit the ginger and add 10 split cardamom pods, adding the pods and seeds to the sliced fruit rinds and diced apricots.

lime jelly marmalade

Makes **about four 1-pint jars**
Preparation time **30 minutes,**
  plus straining
Cooking time **1 hour**
  20 minutes–1 hour
  30 minutes

10 **limes** (about 1½ lb)
6 **lemons** (about 1 lb)
7¾ cups **water**
6¼ cups **granulated sugar**
1 tablespoon **butter** (optional)

Prepare a boiling-water canner (see pages 16–17). Sterilize the jars and lids. Set the screw bands aside.

Pare the rind from the limes and lemons with a vegetable peeler, then cut into fine shreds and set aside. Coarsely chop the peeled fruits and put into a saucepan with 5 cups water. Cover and cook gently for 1 hour or until soft. Meanwhile, add the fruit rinds to a saucepan with the remaining water, bring to a boil, reduce the heat to a simmer, and cook, covered, for 20 minutes, until softened.

Pour the contents of the saucepan through a fine strainer or jelly bag suspended over a large bowl. Let drip for several hours, then squeeze the bag to extract as much juice as possible. Return the strained juice to the pan with the cooked fruit rinds and their cooking liquid. Add the sugar and heat gently, stirring occasionally, until completely dissolved. Bring to a boil, then boil rapidly until setting point is reached (20–30 minutes). Skim with a draining spoon or stir in butter, if needed. Let stand for 10 minutes so that the fruit rinds don't rise when canned.

Ladle into the sterilized jars, working with one at a time. Fill each jar to ¼ inch from the top. Clean the rim and threads of the jar before covering with a lid and securing with a screw band. Repeat with the remaining jars.

Process the filled jars in a boiling-water canner for 5 minutes at sea level (see page 16). Let cool, clean the jars, and label before storing.

For ginger & lemon jelly marmalade, follow the recipe above, but omit the limes and use 9 (2½ lb) lemons, adding a 3-inch piece of ginger root, peeled and finely chopped, with the lemon rinds.

grapefruit jelly marmalade

Makes **about six ½-pint jars**
Preparation time **30 minutes,**
  plus straining
Cooking time **1 hour**
  10 minutes–1 hour
  20 minutes
(not including canning time)

4 **pink grapefruit**
  (about 2½ lb)
7¾ cups **water**
5 cups **granulated sugar**
1 tablespoon **butter** (optional)

Prepare a boiling-water canner (see pages 16–17). Sterilize the jars and lids. Set the screw bands aside.

Peel the grapefruit with a vegetable peeler, then cut the rind into fine shreds and set aside. Coarsely chop the peeled fruits and put into a saucepan with 5 cups water. Cover and cook gently for 1 hour or until soft. Meanwhile, add the fruit rinds to a saucepan, pour in the remaining water, bring to a boil, cover, and simmer gently for 20 minutes, or until tender.

Pour the contents of the saucepan through a fine strainer or jelly bag over a large bowl. Let drip for several hours, then squeeze the bag to extract as much juice as possible. Return the strained juice to the pan with the cooked fruit rinds. Reheat, then add the sugar and heat gently, stirring occasionally, until the sugar has dissolved.

Bring to a boil, then boil rapidly until setting point is reached (10–20 minutes). Skim with a draining spoon or stir in butter, if needed. Leave to cool for 10 minutes so that the fruit rinds will not rise in the jelly when canned.

Ladle into the sterilized jars, working with one at a time. Fill each jar to ¼ inch from the top. Clean the rim and threads of the jar before covering with a lid and securing with a screw band. Repeat with the remaining jars.

Process the filled jars in a boiling-water canner for 5 minutes at sea level (see page 16). Let cool, clean the jars, and label before storing.

To serve, try this marmalade with buttered brioche.

For ruby orange marmalade, make the recipe as above with 2 red-fleshed grapefruit and 4 blood oranges.

lemon & quince marmalade

Makes **about four 1-pint jars**
Preparation time **30 minutes,**
   plus straining
Cooking time **40–50 minutes**
(not including canning time)

5 **lemons** (about 1 lb)
3 lb **quinces**
6½ cups **water**
7½ cups **granulated sugar**
1 tablespoon **butter** (optional)

Prepare a boiling-water canner (see pages 16–17).
Sterilize the jars and lids. Set the screw bands aside.

Peel the lemons with a vegetable peeler and cut the rind
into fine shreds. Squeeze the juice into a bowl. Reserve the
seeds and chop the shells. Peel one-quarter of the quinces,
halve, and core. Cut the flesh into thin strips; add to the
lemon juice. Add the quince peels, core, and seeds to a
saucepan. Chop the remaining quinces, and add to the pan
with the lemon shells and reserved seeds. Add 4¼ cups
water, cover, and cook gently for 30 minutes until soft.

Pour through a jelly bag over a bowl and let drip for
30 minutes, then squeeze the bag to extract 2½ cups
juice. Meanwhile, add the lemon rind, sliced quince,
lemon juice, and remaining water to a small saucepan
and cook, covered, for 20 minutes, until just tender.

Pour the squeezed quince juice back into the pan, and
add the lemon rind, sliced quince, and cooking water. Pour
in the sugar and heat gently, stirring occasionally, until
dissolved. Increase the heat and boil rapidly until setting
point is reached (10–20 minutes). Skim with a draining
spoon or stir in butter, if needed. Let stand for 10 minutes.

Ladle into the sterilized jars, working with one at a time.
Fill each jar to ¼ inch from the top. Clean the rim and
threads of the jar before covering with a lid and securing
with a screw band. Repeat with the remaining jars.

Process the filled jars in a boiling-water canner for
5 minutes at sea level (see page 16). Let cool, clean
the jars, and label before storing.

For lemon & pear marmalade, follow the recipe as
above, but use 9 firm pears (3 lb) instead of quinces.

pineapple marmalade

Makes **about three 1-pint jars**
Preparation time **30 minutes**
Cooking time **50–60 minutes**
(not including canning time)

1 large **pineapple**, trimmed,
    peeled, quartered, and cored
2 **stems lemongrass**
grated rind of 4 **limes**
½ cup freshly squeezed **lime
    juice** (about 3–4 limes)
2 cups **chilled pineapple
    juice** (from a carton)
3¾ cups **granulated sugar**
1 tablespoon **butter** (optional)

Prepare a boiling-water canner (see pages 16–17).
Sterilize the jars and lids. Set the screw bands aside.

Finely chop three-quarters of the pineapple in a food
processor or using a knife. Cut the remaining pineapple
into small cubes. Slit the lemongrass stems and bruise
with a rolling pin, then tie the stems together in the
center with string.

Add the pineapple and lemongrass to a saucepan, then
add the lime rind and juice and the pineapple juice.
Bring to a boil, cover, and simmer gently for 30 minutes.

Pour in the sugar and heat gently, stirring occasionally,
until the sugar has dissolved. Bring to a boil, then boil
rapidly until setting point is reached (20–30 minutes).
Remove the lemongrass. Skim with a draining spoon
or stir in butter, if needed.

Ladle into the sterilized jars, working with one at a time.
Fill each jar to ¼ inch from the top. Clean the rim and
threads of the jar before covering with a lid and securing
with a screw band. Repeat with the remaining jars.

Process the filled jars in a boiling-water canner for
5 minutes at sea level (see page 16). Let cool, clean
the jars, and label before storing.

For pineapple, mango, & lime marmalade, follow
the recipe as above, using ½ large trimmed, peeled,
quartered, and cored pineapple, 2 medium mangoes,
pitted, peeled, and diced, and the lime rind and juice,
but omit the lemongrass.

pressure cooker marmalade

Makes **about four ½-pint jars**
Preparation time **30 minutes**
Cooking time **20–30 minutes**

4 **oranges** (about 1½ lb)
juice of 2 **lemons**
2½ cups **water**
6¼ cups **granulated sugar**
1 tablespoon **butter**

Sterilize the jars and lids.

Halve the oranges and squeeze the juice. Quarter, then scrape away the membrane and pith, leaving a thin layer of pith attached to the rind. Tie the membrane, pith, and seeds in cheesecloth. Thinly slice the orange rind.

Remove the trivet from the pressure cooker. Add the orange rind, orange juice, lemon juice, and cheesecloth bag, then pour in the measured water. Cover with the lid, bring up to medium pressure, then reduce the heat slightly so that the pressure cooker hisses slightly and indicates that the correct pressure has been reached. Cook for 10 minutes, then let cool and allow the pressure to release slowly.

Remove the lid. Lift the cheesecloth bag above the contents in the pressure cooker and press between 2 wooden spoons to remove as much pectin-rich juice as possible; discard the bag. The rind should be just tender; if it is not, bring back to pressure and cook for 2–3 minutes.

Pour in the sugar and heat gently, without the lid, until the sugar has dissolved, stirring occasionally. Bring to a boil, then boil rapidly until setting point is reached (10–20 minutes). Skim with a draining spoon or stir in butter, if needed. Let stand for 10 minutes.

Ladle into sterilized, dry jars, let cool, and cover with lids. Store in the refrigerator for up to 3 weeks.

For orange & lime marmalade, replace the oranges with 1½ lb mixed oranges and limes. Continue as above.

mixed citrus marmalade

Makes **about eight ½-pint jars**
Preparation time **30 minutes**
Cooking time **1 hour**
   10 minutes–1 hour
   20 minutes
(not including canning time)

2 **oranges**
2 **lemons**
2 **limes**
1 **red-fleshed grapefruit**
1 **pink-fleshed grapefruit**
7¾ cups **water**
6¼ cups **granulated sugar**
1 tablespoon **butter** (optional)

Prepare a boiling-water canner (see pages 16–17). Sterilize the jars and lids. Set the screw bands aside.

Peel the fruits with a vegetable peeler, then cut the rind into fine shreds. Add to a saucepan with 2½ cups water, bring to a boil, then cover and simmer gently for 20 minutes, until the rinds are tender. Meanwhile, chop the peeled fruits, put into a saucepan with 5 cups water, cover, and simmer gently for 1 hour, until soft.

Strain the fruit mixture through a fine nylon strainer or jelly bag into a large bowl, pressing the pulp to extract all the juice. Return to the saucepan, stir in the cooked fruit rinds and cooking water, and reheat.

Add the sugar and heat gently, stirring occasionally, until the sugar has dissolved. Bring to a boil, then boil rapidly until setting point is reached (10–20 minutes). Skim with a draining spoon or stir in butter, if needed. Let cool for 10 minutes.

Ladle into the sterilized jars, working with one at a time. Fill each jar to ¼ inch from the top. Clean the rim and threads of the jar before covering with a lid and securing with a screw band. Repeat with the remaining jars.

Process the filled jars in a boiling-water canner for 5 minutes at sea level (see page 16). Let cool, clean the jars, and label before storing.

To serve, try spreading this marmalade over a lemon tart.

For three-fruit shred marmalade, follow the recipe as above, but omit the grapefruit and use 2½ lb mixed oranges, lemons, and limes.

chutneys

mango & pineapple chutney

Makes **about six ½-pint jars**
Preparation time **30 minutes**
Cooking time **20 minutes**
(not including canning time)

1¼ cups **distilled malt
vinegar**
2 cups **granulated sugar**
2 **garlic cloves**, finely chopped
2-inch piece **ginger root**,
peeled and finely chopped
4 **dried chiles**, finely chopped
½ teaspoon **ground allspice**
1 teaspoon **salt**
1 teaspoon mixed
peppercorns, coarsely
crushed
1 large **pineapple**, trimmed,
peeled, cored, and finely
chopped in a food processor
2 large, firm, **unripe mangoes**,
peeled, pitted, and sliced

Prepare a boiling-water canner (see pages 16–17) and heat the cleaned jars and lids in simmering water. Set the screw bands aside.

Add the vinegar, sugar, garlic, and ginger to a large saucepan, then add the dried chiles, allspice, salt, and peppercorns. Heat gently, stirring occasionally, until the sugar has dissolved, then simmer gently for 10 minutes so that the flavors mingle together.

Stir in the pineapple and sliced mango and cook over medium heat for 10 minutes, until the mango is just translucent and the liquid is syrupy.

Ladle into the warmed jars, working with one at a time. Fill each jar to ½ inch from the top, packing down well. Using a plastic spatula, disperse any air bubbles, then clean the rim and threads of the jar before covering with a lid and securing with a screw band. Repeat with the remaining jars.

Process the filled jars in a boiling-water canner for 10 minutes at sea level (see page 16). Let cool, clean the jars, and label before storing.

To serve, partner with poppadums.

For mango & black onion seed chutney, follow the recipe as above, omitting the pineapple. Peel and pit 4 large, firm, unripe mangoes, finely chop 2 of them, and slice the remaining 2. Continue as above, adding 2 tablespoons black onion seeds.

garlicky mediterranean chutney

Makes **about three 1-pint jars**
Preparation time **20 minutes**
Cooking time **1½ hours**

1 **garlic bulb** (about 12 cloves),
   peeled and finely chopped
2 cups chopped **onions**
4 **tomatoes**, skinned (optional)
   and coarsely chopped
4 cups diced **zucchini**
6 **bell peppers** of different
   colors, halved, seeded, and
   cut into strips
1 cup **red wine vinegar**
1¼ cups **granulated sugar**
1 tablespoon **tomato paste**
3 stems **rosemary**, leaves
   chopped
salt and **pepper**

Sterilize the jars and lids, setting the screw bands aside.

Add all the ingredients to a saucepan and cook, uncovered, over gentle heat for 1½ hours, stirring occasionally, but more frequently toward the end of cooking as the chutney thickens.

Ladle into sterilized, dry jars, packing down well and leaving a ½-inch headspace at the top. Disperse any air pockets with a plastic spatula. Cover with the lids, let cool, and store in the refrigerator for up to 3 weeks.

For ratatouille chutney, follow the recipe as above, but reduce the garlic to 4 cloves, and use 3 cups diced zucchini, 4 bell peppers, cored, seeded, and diced, and 1 eggplant, diced. Mix with the onions, tomatoes, vinegar, sugar, rosemary, and tomato paste and continue as above.

eggplant & mint chutney

Makes **about four ½-pint jars**
Preparation time **30 minutes**
Cooking time **1½–1¾ hours**

2 **eggplants** (about 2 lb),
  diced
2 cups chopped **red onions**
4 **tomatoes**, skinned (optional)
  and coarsely chopped
4 cloves **garlic**, finely chopped
1½ cups diced, pitted **dates**
1¼ cups **red wine vinegar**
1 cup firmly packed **light
  brown sugar**
2 teaspoons **coriander seeds**,
  coarsely crushed
2 teaspoons **cumin seeds**,
  coarsely crushed
1 teaspoon **paprika**
1 teaspoon **salt**
¼ cup **chopped mint**

Sterilize the jars and lids, setting the screw bands aside.

Add all the ingredients except the mint to a saucepan, cover, and cook over gentle heat for 1 hour, stirring occasionally, until softened. Remove the lid and cook for 30–45 minutes until thick, stirring more frequently toward the end of cooking as the chutney thickens. Stir the mint into the chutney.

Ladle into sterilized, dry jars, packing down well and leaving a ½-inch headspace at the top. Disperse any air pockets with a plastic spatula. Cover with the lids, let cool, and store in the refrigerator for up to 3 weeks.

To serve, this chutney is delicious as a mezze appetizer with olives, marinated peppers, yogurt mixed with chopped mint, and grilled pita bread.

For eggplant & chile chutney, add 1–2 large mild red chiles, to taste, finely chopped and seeds discarded, when adding the garlic. Stir ¼ cup chopped cilantro into the cooked chutney instead of the mint.

ale, apple, & mustard chutney

Makes **about eight**
  ½-pint jars
Preparation time **30 minutes**
Cooking time **1¾–2 hours**
(not including canning time)

6 **cooking apples** (about 2 lb),
  quartered, cored, peeled,
  and diced
3 cups finely chopped **onions**
2 cups diced **celery**
1¾ cups diced, pitted **dates**
2½ cups **brown ale**
⅔ cup **distilled malt vinegar**
1⅓ cups firmly packed **brown
  sugar**
2 tablespoons **white mustard**
  seeds, coarsely crushed
1 teaspoon **turmeric**
1 teaspoon **salt**
1 teaspoon **peppercorns**,
  coarsely crushed

Prepare a boiling-water canner (see pages 16–17) and heat the cleaned jars and lids in simmering water. Set the screw bands aside.

Add all the ingredients to a saucepan and cook, uncovered, over gentle heat for 1¾–2 hours, stirring occasionally, but more frequently toward the end of cooking as the chutney thickens.

Ladle into the warmed jars, working with one at a time. Fill each jar to ½ inch from the top, packing down well. Using a plastic spatula, disperse any air bubbles, then clean the rim and threads of the jar before covering with a lid and securing with a screw band. Repeat with the remaining jars.

Process the filled jars in a boiling-water canner for 15 minutes at sea level (see page 16). Let cool, clean the jars, and label before storing.

To serve, this chutney is delicious served with apples, cheese, and thick slices of bread.

For apple & ginger beer chutney, follow the recipe as above, but replace the ale with ginger beer and add golden raisins in place of the dates.

autumnal harvest chutney

Makes **about six 1-pint jars**
Preparation time **30 minutes**
Cooking time **1½ hours**

8 mixed **green** and **red**
   tomatoes (about 2 lb),
   coarsely chopped
8 **red plums** (about 1 lb),
   pitted and coarsely chopped
1 large, overgrown **zucchini**
   (about 1½ lb), peeled,
   halved, seeded, and diced
3 cups coarsely chopped
   onions
⅔ cup **golden raisins** or
   raisins
1¼ cups **distilled malt**
   vinegar
1¼ cups **granulated sugar**
1 tablespoon **tomato paste**
2 teaspoons **hot paprika**
2 teaspoons **English mustard**
   powder
1 teaspoon **salt**
2 teaspoons **peppercorns**,
   coarsely crushed

Sterilize the jars and lids, setting the screw bands aside.

Add all the ingredients to a saucepan, stir to combine,
then cook, uncovered, over a gentle heat for 1½ hours,
stirring occasionally, but more frequently toward the end
of cooking as the chutney thickens.

Ladle into sterilized, dry jars, packing down well and
leaving a ½-inch headspace at the top. Disperse any
air pockets with a plastic spatula. Cover with the lids,
let cool, and store in the refrigerator for up to 3 weeks.

For apple & tomato chutney, follow the recipe as
above, but omit the plums and add 3 peeled, cored,
and diced cooking apples (about 1 lb).

green bean chutney

Makes **about six 1-pint jars**
Preparation time **25 minutes**
Cooking time **about
   35 minutes**

10 cups trimmed **green beans**
   (about 2 lb)
3¾ cups **distilled malt
   vinegar**
3½ cups firmly packed
   brown sugar
3 cups chopped **onions**
1½ tablespoons **turmeric**
1½ tablespoons **mustard
   powder**
3 tablespoons **black
   mustard seeds**
3 tablespoons **cornstarch**
1 teaspoon **salt**
pepper
3 tablespoons **water**

Sterilize the jars and lids, setting the screw bands aside.

Fill a saucepan halfway with water, bring to a boil, then add the green beans. Return to a boil and cook for 3 minutes. Drain into a colander, refresh with cold water, then drain again. Thinly slice the beans or coarsely chop in a food processor.

Add the vinegar and sugar to the drained saucepan, then add the onions. Cover and bring to a boil, then reduce the heat and simmer for 10 minutes.

Mix together the remaining dry ingredients in a bowl, then stir in the measured water until smooth. Stir this into the vinegar mixture, then simmer, uncovered, for 10 minutes, stirring until smooth and thickened.

Stir the blanched beans into the vinegar mixture and cook gently for 10 minutes, stirring frequently until just tender.

Ladle into sterilized, dry jars, packing down well and leaving a ½-inch headspace at the top. Disperse any air pockets with a plastic spatula. Cover with the lids, let cool, and store in the refrigerator for up to 3 weeks.

For zucchini & mixed bean chutney, blanch 7½ cups mixed green, black, and yellow snap beans (about 1½ lb) as above, then drain and chop. Add to the cooked vinegar and onion mixture with 2 cups diced zucchini. Continue as above.

green tomato chutney

Makes **about eight**
½-pint jars
Preparation time **15 minutes**
Cooking time 1¼–1½ **hours**
(not including canning time)

8 **green tomatoes**
   (about 2 lb), finely chopped
3 cups finely chopped **onions**,
3 **cooking apples**, peeled,
   cored, and chopped
2 **fresh green chiles**,
   halved, seeded, and
   finely chopped
2 **garlic cloves**, crushed
1 teaspoon **ground ginger**
generous pinch of **ground**
   clove
generous pinch of **ground**
   turmeric
⅓ cup **raisins**
1 cup firmly packed **dark**
   brown sugar
1¼ cups **white wine vinegar**

Prepare a boiling-water canner (see pages 16–17) and heat the cleaned jars and lids in simmering water. Set the screw bands aside.

Add the tomatoes, onions, apples, and chiles to a large saucepan and mix together. Add the garlic, ginger, ground clove, and turmeric, then stir in the raisins, sugar, and vinegar.

Bring to a boil, then reduce the heat and simmer, covered, for 1¼–1½ hours, or until the chutney has thickened, stirring frequently.

Ladle into the warmed jars, working with one at a time. Fill each jar to ½ inch from the top, packing down well. Using a plastic spatula, disperse any air bubbles, then clean the rim and threads of the jar before covering with a lid and securing with a screw band. Repeat with the remaining jars.

Process the filled jars in a boiling-water canner for 15 minutes at sea level (see page 16). Let cool, clean the jars, and label before storing.

For green tomato & mango chutney, follow the recipe as above, but peel 1 large, ripe mango and cut the flesh from the pit. Dice the flesh and add this in place of the apples to the green tomatoes and onions. Add the chiles, spices, and ¾ cup chopped dried apricots with the sugar and vinegar.

pumpkin & walnut chutney

Makes **about eight**
 ½-pint jars
Preparation time **30 minutes**
Cooking time **1½–2 hours**
(not including canning time)

8 cups peeled, seeded, and
 diced **pie pumpkin** or
 winter squash
2 **onions**, finely chopped
1 large **orange**, finely chopped,
 including skin and pith
2½ cups **white wine vinegar**
2 cups **granulated sugar**
1 **cinnamon stick**, halved
2-inch piece **ginger root**,
 peeled and finely chopped
1 teaspoon **turmeric**
1 teaspoon **dried red pepper
 flakes**
1 teaspoon **salt**
a little **pepper**
½ cup **walnut pieces**

Prepare a boiling-water canner (see pages 16–17) and heat the cleaned jars and lids in simmering water. Set the screw bands aside.

Add the pumpkin to a saucepan with all the remaining ingredients. Cover and cook gently for 1 hour, stirring occasionally, until softened. Remove the lid and cook for ½–1 hour, stirring more frequently toward the end of cooking as the chutney thickens.

Ladle into the warmed jars, working with one at a time. Fill each jar to ½ inch from the top, packing down well. Using a plastic spatula, disperse any air bubbles, then clean the rim and threads of the jar before covering with a lid and securing with a screw band. Repeat with the remaining jars.

Process the filled jars in a boiling-water canner for 15 minutes at sea level (see page 16). Let cool, clean the jars, and label before storing.

For pumpkin & date chutney, follow the recipe as above, but omit the walnut pieces and add 1 cup diced pitted dates instead.

pumpkin & red bell pepper chutney

Makes **about six ½-pint jars**
Preparation time **30 minutes**
Cooking time **1¼ hours**

2 lb sliced **pie pumpkin**, or
  winter squash, weighed
  after peeling and seeding
2 **red bell peppers**, quartered,
  seeded, and cored
1 lb **shallots**, peeled,
  halved if large
3 **bay leaves**
3 tablespoons **olive oil**
1¾ cups **hard cider** or **white
  wine vinegar**
⅔ cup **granulated sugar**
½ cup firmly packed **light
  brown sugar**
1 teaspoon **allspice berries**,
  coarsely crushed
½ teaspoon **salt**
½ teaspoon **cayenne pepper**

Preheat the oven to 400°F.

Sterilize the jars and lids, setting the screw bands aside.

Add the pumpkin, bell peppers, and shallots to a large roasting pan. Tuck the bay leaves in among the vegetables, then drizzle with the oil. Roast in the preheated oven, for 45 minutes, until the vegetables are tender and browned.

Let cool slightly, then remove the skins from the bell peppers. Coarsely chop the bell peppers, pumpkin, and shallots, and discard the bay leaves. Add the vegetables and any juices from the roasting pan to a saucepan. Add all the remaining ingredients, then bring to a boil and simmer, uncovered, for about 30 minutes, stirring more frequently toward the end of cooking, until thick.

Ladle into sterilized, dry jars, packing down well and leaving a ½-inch headspace at the top. Disperse any air pockets with a plastic spatula. Cover with the lids, let cool, and store in the refrigerator for up to 3 weeks.

For roasted root chutney, slice 4 peeled parsnips and 3 sweet potatoes (about 2 lb total), then roast with the shallots and red bell peppers. Continue as above, adding 1 teaspoon turmeric and 1 teaspoon smoked paprika instead of the allspice berries.

cayenne pepper & garlic chutney

Makes **about four ½-pint jars**
Preparation time **15 minutes**
Cooking time **30 minutes**

1 lb **fresh cayenne peppers**,
   red or green
6 **garlic cloves**, crushed
¼ cup **ground cumin**
2 tablespoons **ground
   turmeric**
1 large **onion**, finely chopped
1 tablespoon **salt**
¼ cup grated **ginger root**
1¼ cups **peanut oil**
3 tablespoons **brown sugar**
1¼ cups **white wine vinegar**

Sterilize the jars and lids, setting the screw bands aside.

Remove the stems from the chiles, then finely chop the chiles, seeds and all.

Add the chiles, garlic, cumin, turmeric, onion, salt, ginger, and oil to a large saucepan and sauté for 15 minutes, stirring frequently. Add the sugar and vinegar and bring to a boil. Reduce the heat to medium and simmer, covered, for 10 minutes, stirring occasionally.

Ladle into sterilized, dry jars, packing down well and leaving a ½-inch headspace at the top. Disperse any air pockets with a plastic spatula. Cover with the lids, let cool, and store in the refrigerator for up to 3 weeks.

To serve, partner this chutney with curry.

For hot chile & tamarind chutney, follow the recipe as above, reducing the cumin to 2 tablespoons and adding 1 tablespoon tamarind paste and the grated rind and juice of 1 lime.

chestnut, onion, & fennel chutney

Makes **about two ½-pint jars**
Preparation time **15 minutes**
Cooking time **1 hour**
  25 minutes–1 hour
  30 minutes

¼ cup **olive oil**
4 large **red onions**, thinly
  sliced
1 **fennel bulb**, trimmed and
  thinly sliced
2 cups halved **cooked,
  peeled chestnuts**
½ cup firmly packed **light
  brown sugar**
½ cup **cider vinegar**
½ cup **sweet sherry** or
  marsala wine
pepper

Sterilize the jars and lids, setting the screw bands aside.

Heat the oil in a large saucepan, add the onions and fennel, and cook over gentle heat for 25–30 minutes, until the onions are soft.

Add the chestnuts, sugar, vinegar, and sherry or marsala to the pan, season well with pepper, and stir. Simmer gently, uncovered, for about 1 hour, stirring occasionally, until the chutney has thickened.

Ladle into sterilized, dry jars, packing down well and leaving a ½-inch headspace at the top. Disperse any air pockets with a plastic spatula. Cover with the lids, let cool, and store in the refrigerator for up to 3 weeks.

To serve, this chutney goes well with rustic bread topped with blue cheese.

For red onion & raisin chutney, sauté 6 sliced red onions (about 3 lb) in 3 tablespoons olive oil for 10 minutes. Stir in 2 tablespoons light brown sugar, sauté gently for 15 minutes, until browned, then stir in an extra 1 cup firmly packed light brown sugar, 1¼ cups red wine vinegar, 1⅓ cups raisins, 3 chopped garlic cloves, 3 bay leaves, 1 tablespoon whole-grain mustard, salt, and pepper. Simmer gently for 30 minutes, until thick, then ladle into sterilized jars as above.

peach & date chutney

Makes **about three to four
½-pint jars**
Preparation time **10 minutes**
Cooking time **50 minutes**
(not including canning time)

12 **peaches**
3 **onions**, finely chopped
2 **garlic cloves**, crushed
2 tablespoons **grated root
ginger**
1 cup chopped **pitted dates**
1 ¼ cups **demerara sugar** or
other **raw sugar**
1 ¼ cups **red wine vinegar**
salt and **pepper**

Prepare a boiling-water canner (see pages 16–17) and
heat the cleaned jars and lids in simmering water. Set the
screw bands aside.

Place the peaches in a large bowl, cover with boiling
water, and let stand for about 1 minute, then drain and
peel. Halve and pit the fruit and cut into thick slices.

Add the onions to a pan with the peaches, garlic, ginger,
dates, sugar, and vinegar. Add a generous sprinkling of
salt and pepper and bring to a boil, stirring continuously,
until the sugar has completely dissolved.

Reduce the heat and simmer, covered, stirring frequently,
for 45 minutes, until the chutney has thickened.

Ladle into the warmed jars, working with one at a time.
Fill each jar to ½ inch from the top, packing down well.
Using a plastic spatula, disperse any air bubbles, then
clean the rim and threads of the jar before covering with
a lid and securing with a screw band. Repeat with the
remaining jars.

Process the filled jars in a boiling-water canner for
15 minutes at sea level (see page 16). Let cool, clean
the jars, and label before storing.

For peach & orange chutney, finely chop 1 whole
orange and add this to a saucepan with the onions,
peaches, ginger, sugar, and seasoning, as above,
then add 1 cup shredded carrot and 1 ¼ cups white
wine vinegar.

carrot & cilantro chutney

Makes **about four 1-pint jars**
Preparation time **25 minutes**
Cooking time **1–1¼ hours**

9 cups shredded **carrots**
   (about 2 lb)
1 **onion**, chopped
1 large **cooking apple**,
   quartered, cored, peeled,
   and diced
1½-inch piece **ginger root**,
   peeled and finely chopped
4 **garlic cloves**, finely chopped
¾ cup **golden raisins**
4¼ cups **distilled**
   malt vinegar
1¼ cups **granulated sugar**
2 teaspoons **curry powder**
2 teaspoons **black mustard**
   seeds (optional)
½ teaspoon **salt**
pepper
small bunch of **cilantro**,
   coarsely chopped

Sterilize the jars and lids, setting the screw bands aside.

Add all the ingredients, except the cilantro, to a saucepan. Bring to a boil, then simmer, uncovered, for 1–1¼ hours, stirring occasionally, until the chutney is thick.

Remove from the heat and stir in the cilantro.

Ladle into sterilized, dry jars, packing down well and leaving a ½-inch headspace at the top. Disperse any air pockets with a plastic spatula. Cover with the lids, let cool, and store in the refrigerator for up to 3 weeks.

For gingered parsnip & cilantro chutney, omit the carrots and add 6 peeled and grated parsnips (about 2 lb), using 1 teaspoon dried red pepper flakes instead of the mustard seeds. Continue as above.

sweet potato & orange chutney

Makes **about 10 ½-pint jars**
Preparation time **30 minutes**
Cooking time **1¾–2 hours**

4 **sweet potatoes** (1½ lb),
   peeled and diced
3 cups chopped **onions**
1⅔ cups **golden raisins**
2¼ cups shredded **carrots**
2 **oranges**, finely chopped,
   including pith and peel
4 **garlic cloves**, finely chopped
⅓ cup **tamarind pulp**
1⅓ cups firmly packed **light
   brown sugar**
3 cups **distilled malt vinegar**
1½ teaspoons **dried red
   pepper flakes**
1 teaspoon **salt**
1 teaspoon **black pepper**,
   coarsely crushed

Sterilize the jars and lids, setting the screw bands aside.

Add all the ingredients to a saucepan, cover, and cook gently for 1 hour, stirring occasionally. Remove the lid and cook for ¾–1 hour, stirring more frequently toward the end of cooking as the chutney thickens.

Ladle into sterilized, dry jars, packing down well and leaving a ½-inch headspace at the top. Disperse any air pockets with a plastic spatula. Cover with the lids, let cool, and store in the refrigerator for up to 3 weeks.

To serve, this chutney will enhance any cheeseboard.

For sweet potato, ginger, & orange chutney, follow the recipe as above, but omit the tamarind and add a 2-inch piece of peeled, finely chopped ginger root.

andrew's plums

Makes **about four ½-pint jars**
Preparation time **25 minutes**
Cooking time **1 hour**
(not including canning time)

½ teaspoon **cumin seeds**
½ teaspoon **fennel seeds**
1 teaspoon **coriander seeds**
½ teaspoon **dried red pepper flakes**
1 quart **plums** (about 2 lb), halved, pitted, and diced
1 **onion**, chopped
1-inch piece **ginger root**, peeled and finely chopped
⅔ cup **malt vinegar**
⅔ cup **granulated sugar**
2 tablespoons **raisins**
juice of 1 **lemon**
salt and **pepper**

Prepare a boiling-water canner (see pages 16–17) and heat the cleaned jars and lids in simmering water. Set the screw bands aside.

Crush all the seeds coarsely in a mortar and pestle, then toast in a hot saucepan with the red pepper flakes for a few seconds. Add all the remaining ingredients, then cover and simmer gently for 30 minutes, stirring occasionally.

Uncover the chutney and cook for 30 minutes, stirring until thick and pulpy. Mash with a vegetable masher, or process in a food processor or blender until smooth.

Ladle into the warmed jars, working with one at a time. Fill each jar to ½ inch from the top, packing down well. Using a plastic spatula, disperse any air bubbles, then clean the rim and threads of the jar before covering with a lid and securing with a screw band. Repeat with the remaining jars.

Process the filled jars in a boiling-water canner for 15 minutes at sea level (see page 16). Let cool, clean the jars, and label before storing.

To serve, try adding to a cheese, lettuce, and tomato sandwich.

For smooth plum & tomato chutney, follow the recipe as above, but use 1 lb plums, pitted and diced, along with 4 coarsely chopped tomatoes.

relishes

chile & red tomato relish

Makes **about six ½-pint jars**
Preparation time **25 minutes**
Cooking time **1 hour
    5 minutes**
(not including canning time)

2 tablespoons **sunflower oil**
3 cups finely chopped **onions**
8 **tomatoes** (about 2 lb),
    skinned (optional) and
    coarsely chopped
4 **red finger chiles**, seeded
    and chopped
3 stems **fresh thyme**
2 tablespoons **tomato paste**
1 teaspoon **smoked paprika**
1¼ cups **distilled
    malt vinegar**
1¼ cups **granulated sugar**
salt and **pepper**

Prepare a boiling-water canner (see pages 16–17) and heat the cleaned jars and lids in simmering water. Set the screw bands aside.

Heat the oil in a saucepan, add the onions, and sauté for 5 minutes, until softened. Stir in the tomatoes and chiles, then add the remaining ingredients.

Cook, uncovered, for 1 hour, stirring more frequently toward the end of cooking as the relish thickens.

Ladle into the warmed jars, working with one at a time. Fill each jar to ½ inch from the top. Using a plastic spatula, disperse any air bubbles, then clean the rim and threads of the jar before covering with a lid and securing with a screw band. Repeat with the remaining jars.

Process the filled jars in a boiling-water canner for 20 minutes at sea level (see page 16). Let cool, clean the jars, and label before storing for 3 weeks before using.

To serve, this relish goes well with Chinese-style pancake rolls, shrimp sesame toast, and tiny dumplings.

For jerked tomato relish, crush 1 teaspoon allspice berries and 1 teaspoon black peppercorns and add to the ingredients above, along with ½ teaspoon ground cinnamon, 2 cloves garlic, finely chopped, and the grated rind and juice of 1 lime.

gooseberry relish with cardamom

Makes **four ½-pint jars**
Preparation time **25 minutes**
Cooking time **45 minutes**
(not including canning time)

6½ cups trimmed
   gooseberries (about 2 lb)
2 **onions**, chopped
10 **cardamom pods**, crushed
1¼ cups **distilled**
   malt vinegar
1¼ cups **granulated sugar**
1 teaspoon **salt**
pepper

Prepare a boiling-water canner (see pages 16–17). Sterilize the jars and lids. Set the screw bands aside.

Add all the ingredients to a saucepan.

Cook gently, uncovered, for 45 minutes, until the gooseberries are soft, stirring occasionally, but more frequently toward the end of cooking as the relish thickens.

Ladle into the sterilized jars, working with one at a time. Fill each jar to ½ inch from the top. Using a plastic spatula, disperse any air bubbles, then clean the rim and threads of the jar before covering with a lid and securing with a screw band. Repeat with the remaining jars.

Process the filled jars in a boiling-water canner for 5 minutes at sea level (see page 16). Let cool, clean the jars, and label. Store for 3 weeks before using.

To serve, this relish is tasty with pork pie, lettuce, and scallions.

For spiced peach relish, omit the gooseberries and add 6 peaches (about 2 lb), pitted and finely diced. Cook with the onion, cardamom pods, a 2-inch cinnamon stick, and 4 cloves as above, and process in the water bath for 15 minutes at sea level.

sweet chile & kaffir lime relish

Makes **about three to four ½-pint jars**
Preparation time **25 minutes**
Cooking time **1 hour**

3 cups finely chopped **onions,**
4 **limes**, finely chopped, including pith and peel
6 **green cayenne chiles**, including seeds, chopped
2 **green bell peppers**, cored, seeded, and diced
1 tablespoon **black mustard seeds**
1 teaspoon **turmeric**
4 **kaffir lime leaves**
²/₃ cup **distilled malt vinegar**
2½ cups **granulated sugar**
1 teaspoon **salt**
pepper

Sterilize the jars and lids, setting the screw bands aside.

Add all the ingredients to a saucepan, cover, and simmer gently for 45 minutes, stirring from time to time.

Remove the lid and cook for another 15 minutes, until the limes are soft, stirring more frequently toward the end of cooking as the relish thickens.

Ladle into sterilized jars, packing down well, and disperse any air pockets with a plastic spatula. Cover with the lids, let cool, and store in the refrigerator for 3 weeks before using.

For South Seas relish, add 1½ cups finely chopped onions, 1½ cups finely chopped fresh pineapple, 4 limes (including the pith and peel), chopped, 6 green cayenne chiles, finely chopped, 1 red and 1 green bell pepper, cored, seeded, and finely chopped, to a saucepan with 1 teaspoon turmeric, 1 teaspoon allspice berries, coarsely crushed, plus the vinegar, sugar, salt, and pepper as above. Continue as above.

apple & tomato relish

Makes **four ½-pint jars**
Preparation time **20 minutes**
Cooking time **1 hour
  5 minutes**
(not including canning time)

2 tablespoons **sunflower oil**
2 **onions**, coarsely chopped
2 **Granny Smith** or other sharp
  apples, quartered, cored,
  peeled, and diced
8 **tomatoes** (about 2 lb),
  skinned (optional) and
  coarsely chopped
1 ¼ cups **distilled
  malt vinegar**
1 ¼ cups **granulated sugar**
2 tablespoons **tomato paste**
1 tablespoon **Worcestershire
  sauce**
1 teaspoon **paprika**
2 **bay leaves**
salt and **pepper**

Prepare a boiling-water canner (see pages 16–17) and heat the cleaned jars and lids in simmering water. Set the screw bands aside.

Heat the oil in a saucepan, add the onions, and sauté for 5 minutes, until softened. Add the apples and tomatoes, then stir in the remaining ingredients.

Cook over and gentle heat, uncovered, for 1 hour, stirring more frequently toward the end of cooking as the relish thickens.

Ladle into the sterilized jars, working with one at a time. Fill each jar to ½ inch from the top. Using a plastic spatula, disperse any air bubbles, then clean the rim and threads of the jar before covering with a lid and securing with a screw band. Repeat with the remaining jars.

Process the filled jars in a boiling-water canner for 10 minutes at sea level (see page 16). Let cool, clean the jars, and label. Store for 3 weeks before using.

To serve, this relish is perfect for dipping chunky fries.

For garlicky tomato relish, add 4 finely chopped garlic cloves to the saucepan and cook as above.

cucumber & bell pepper relish

Makes **about six ½-pint jars**
Preparation time **30 minutes,**
  plus soaking
Cooking time **25 minutes**
(not including canning time)

2 **cucumbers**, diced
¼ cup **salt**
1 tablespoon **sunflower oil**
2 **onions**, chopped
2 **red bell peppers**, cored,
  seeded, and diced
1¼ cups **distilled**
  malt vinegar
1½ cups **granulated sugar**
1 teaspoon **dried**
  red pepper flakes
½ teaspoon **turmeric**
2 teaspoons **mustard powder**
2 tablespoons **cornstarch**
2 tablespoons **water**
½ teaspoon **peppercorns**,
  coarsely crushed

Layer the cucumbers in a bowl with the salt, cover with a plate, weigh down, and let soak for 4 hours. Transfer to a colander, drain, rinse with cold water, and drain well.

Prepare a boiling-water canner (see pages 16–17) and heat the cleaned jars and lids in simmering water. Set the screw bands aside.

Heat the oil in a saucepan, add the onions, and sauté for 5 minutes, stirring until softened. Add the bell peppers and sauté for another 5 minutes. Add the vinegar and sugar to the pan. Mix the red pepper flakes, turmeric, mustard powder, and cornstarch in a bowl, then stir in the measured water and mix until smooth. Stir into the vinegar mixture and mix until smooth. Cook gently for 10 minutes, stirring occasionally, until thickened. Stir in the cucumber and peppercorns and cook for 5 minutes.

Ladle into the sterilized jars, working with one at a time. Fill each jar to ½ inch from the top. Using a plastic spatula, disperse any air bubbles, then clean the rim and threads of the jar before covering with a lid and securing with a screw band. Repeat with the remaining jars.

Process the filled jars in a boiling-water canner for 10 minutes at sea level (see page 16). Let cool, clean the jars, and label. Store for 3 weeks before using.

For mixed bell pepper relish, halve 2 red, 2 green, and 2 orange bell peppers, remove the seeds and core, then finely chop. Sauté 1 chopped onion in 1 tablespoon sunflower oil until softened. Add the chopped peppers and cook for 5 minutes. Add the vinegar and sugar, then mix the spices with cornstarch and finish as above.

beet & apple relish

Makes **about six ½-pint jars**
Preparation time **15 minutes**
Cooking time about **1½ hours**
(not including canning time)

3 **cooking apples**, peeled,
   halved, and cored
6 **beets** (about 1 lb), peeled
2 cups finely chopped **onions**
1 tablespoon finely chopped
   ginger root
2 large **garlic cloves**, crushed
1 teaspoon **paprika**
1 teaspoon **ground turmeric**
1 **cinnamon stick**
1 cup firmly packed **dark
   brown sugar**
2 cups **red wine vinegar**

Prepare a boiling-water canner (see pages 16–17) and heat the cleaned jars and lids in simmering water. Set the screw bands aside.

Grate the apples and beets into a large saucepan, then add all the remaining ingredients.

Bring to a boil, then reduce the heat and simmer, covered, stirring occasionally, for about 1½ hours, until the relish has thickened and the beets are tender.

Ladle into the sterilized jars, working with one at a time. Fill each jar to ½ inch from the top. Using a plastic spatula, disperse any air bubbles, then clean the rim and threads of the jar before covering with a lid and securing with a screw band. Repeat with the remaining jars.

Process the filled jars in a boiling-water canner for 10 minutes at sea level (see page 16). Let cool, clean the jars, and label. Store for 1 week before using.

To serve, partner this relish with pork chops.

For beet & horseradish relish, omit the turmeric and cinnamon and stir in a 2-inch raw horseradish root, peeled and grated. Continue as above.

colorful corn relish

Makes **about six ½-pint jars**
Preparation time **15 minutes**
Cooking time **25 minutes**
(not including canning time)

¼ cup **corn oil**
2 large **onions**, finely chopped
1 **green bell pepper**, cored,
    seeded, and finely chopped
1 **red bell pepper**, cored,
    seeded, and finely chopped
4 **celery sticks**, finely chopped
1 teaspoon **salt**
1 large **garlic clove**, crushed
2 **carrots**, peeled and cut into
    small cubes
¼ cup **sugar**
2 teaspoons **mustard powder**
4½ cups **frozen corn kernels**
2 cups **vinegar**

Prepare a boiling-water canner (see pages 16–17) and heat the cleaned jars and lids in simmering water. Set the screw bands aside.

Heat the oil in a large saucepan and add the onions, bell peppers, and celery. Sauté gently for 10 minutes, until soft but not browned, then add the salt and garlic.

Add all the remaining ingredients and bring to a boil. Reduce the heat and cook, uncovered, for 15 minutes, stirring occasionally.

Ladle into the sterilized jars, working with one at a time. Fill each jar to ½ inch from the top. Using a plastic spatula, disperse any air bubbles, then clean the rim and threads of the jar before covering with a lid and securing with a screw band. Repeat with the remaining jars.

Process the filled jars in a boiling-water canner for 10 minutes at sea level (see page 16). Let cool, clean the jars, and label before storing.

To serve, this relish makes a great accompaniment to homemade burgers.

For hot corn relish, add 1 teaspoon smoked paprika and 1 teaspoon dried red pepper flakes when stirring in the vinegar.

tomato & bell pepper relish

Makes **eight ½-pint jars**

Preparation time **20 minutes**

Cooking time **about
30 minutes**

(not including canning time)

8 **ripe tomatoes** (about 2 lb),
skinned and chopped

8 **red bell peppers** (about
2 lb), cored, seeded, and
finely chopped

3 cups finely chopped **onions**

2 **red chiles**, seeded and
finely chopped

2 cups **red wine vinegar**

¾ cup firmly packed **light
brown sugar**

¼ cup **mustard seeds**

2 tablespoons **celery seeds**

1 tablespoon **paprika**

2 teaspoons **salt**

2 teaspoons **pepper**

Prepare a boiling-water canner (see pages 16–17) and heat the cleaned jars and lids in simmering water. Set the screw bands aside.

Combine all the ingredients in a large saucepan.

Bring the mixture to a boil over moderate heat, then reduce the heat and simmer, uncovered, for about 30 minutes, until most of the liquid has evaporated and the relish has a thick, pulpy consistency. Stir frequently as the relish thickens.

Ladle into the sterilized jars, working with one at a time. Fill each jar to ½ inch from the top. Using a plastic spatula, disperse any air bubbles, then clean the rim and threads of the jar before covering with a lid and securing with a screw band. Repeat with the remaining jars.

Process the filled jars in a boiling-water canner for 15 minutes at sea level (see page 16). Let cool, clean the jars, and label. Store for 3 weeks before using.

For tomato & eggplant relish, replace the bell pepper with 2 medium eggplants (about 2 lb) cut into small dice, and 2 tablespoons tomato paste, then continue as above.

pickles

pickled peaches

Makes **about one 1-pint jar**
Preparation time **25 minutes**
Cooking time **6–8 minutes**

1 ¼ cups **distilled white
  vinegar**
2 ½ cups **granulated sugar**
1 teaspoon **whole cloves**
1 teaspoon **whole allspice
  berries**
3-inch **cinnamon stick**, halved
6 **small peaches** (about 2 lb),
  halved and pitted

Sterilize the jar and lid, setting the screw band aside.

Pour the vinegar into a large saucepan, add the sugar and spices, and heat gently until the sugar has dissolved.

Add the peach halves and cook gently for 4–5 minutes, until just tender but still firm. Lift out of the syrup with a slotted spoon and pack tightly into the sterilized jar.

Boil the syrup for 2–3 minutes to concentrate the flavors, then pour over the fruit, making sure that the fruit is completely covered and the jar filled to the very top. Top up with a little extra warm vinegar, if needed. Add a small piece of crumpled wax paper to stop the fruit from rising out of the vinegar in the jar. Let cool, cover with the lid, and label.

After a few hours, the peaches will begin to rise in the jar, but as they become saturated with the syrup, they will sink once more; at this point, they will be ready to eat. Store in the refrigerator for up to 3 weeks.

To serve, these peaches go well with slices of ham.

For pickled peach dressing, whisk 2 tablespoons spiced syrup from the jar of peaches with 3 tablespoons olive oil and 2 tablespoons finely chopped parsley or chives, then toss with 3 ½ cups salad greens.

preserved lemons

Makes **about one 1-pint jar**
Preparation time **10 minutes**

8 **unwaxed baby lemons**
1 teaspoon **coriander seeds**
1 small **cinnamon stick**,
  bruised
2 **bay leaves**
¼ cup **pickling salt**
juice of 1 **lemon**

Sterilize the jar and lid, setting the screw band aside.

Sprinkle a little salt into the bottom of the sterilized jar, then layer the lemons, spices, bay leaves, and remaining salt in the jar.

Add any remaining salt, the lemon juice, and enough boiling water to cover the lemons. Cover with the lid and let stand in a warm place for a couple of days, then store in the refrigerator for at least 3 weeks before using, so that the lemon skins soften. Use within 6 months, and rinse off before using.

For pickled lemons with chile & garlic, tuck 4 dried chiles into the jar with 8 unpeeled cloves of garlic and the lemons, and continue as above.

lime pickle

Makes **about one 1-pint jar**
Preparation time **10 minutes**
Cooking time **5 minutes**

10 **limes**, each cut into
  6 wedges
¼ cup **pickling salt**
1 tablespoon **fenugreek
  seeds**
1 tablespoon **black mustard
  seeds**
1 tablespoon **chile powder**
1 tablespoon **ground turmeric**
1¼ cups **vegetable oil**
½ teaspoon **ground
  asafetida** (available in
  Asian grocery stores)

Sterilize the jar and lid, setting the screw band aside.

Put the limes into the sterilized, dry jar—make sure the jar and everything else used for making the recipe remains dry—and cover with the salt.

Dry-fry the fenugreek and mustard seeds in a small nonstick skillet, then grind them to a powder in either a mortar with a pestle, spice grinder, or coffee grinder kept specially for the purpose.

Add the ground seeds, chile powder, and turmeric to the limes and mix well.

Heat the oil in a small skillet until smoking, add the asafetida, and sauté for 30 seconds. Pour the oil over the limes and mix well.

Cover the jar with the lid and let stand in a bright, warm place for 10 days to mature. Store in the refrigerator for a few weeks before using.

For pickled kumquats, halve 30 kumquats and pack into a jar with the salt as above. Dry-fry 1 tablespoon coriander seeds with 2 teaspoons cumin seeds, coarsely grind in a mortar and pestle, mix with 1 teaspoon dried chile seeds, 1 teaspoon turmeric, and 1 teaspoon smoked paprika, then stir in 1¼ cups vegetable oil and pour over the kumquats. Continue as above.

sweet pickled cucumbers

Makes **about three 1-pint jars**
Preparation time **25 minutes,**
  plus soaking
Cooking time **5–6 minutes**

2 large unwaxed **cucumbers**,
  thinly sliced
1 medium **onion**, thinly sliced
¼ cup **salt**
2 cups **white wine vinegar**
2 cups **granulated sugar**
½ teaspoon **turmeric**
2 teaspoons **fennel seeds**
½ teaspoon **dried red pepper**
  flakes
¼ teaspoon **peppercorns**,
  coarsely crushed

Layer the cucumbers, onions, and salt in a bowl, cover with a plate, and weigh down, then let soak for 4 hours.

Meanwhile, sterilize the jars and lids, setting the screw bands aside.

Pour the vinegar into a saucepan, add the sugar and the remaining ingredients, and heat gently, stirring occasionally, until the sugar has dissolved, then let cool.

Transfer the cucumber and onions to a colander and drain off the liquid. Rinse with plenty of cold water and drain well.

Reheat the vinegar mixture until just boiling, add the drained cucumber and onion, cook for 1 minute, then lift out of the vinegar with a draining spoon and pack into sterilized, dry jars. Boil the remaining vinegar mixture for 4–5 minutes until syrupy, then let cool.

Pour the cold vinegar mixture over the cucumber slices to completely cover (adding a little extra vinegar if needed). Cover with the lids, label, and let mature in the refrigerator for 3–4 weeks. Use within 3 months.

For sweet pickled oranges, thinly slice 6 thin-skinned oranges, put into a saucepan, cover with water, and bring to a boil. Simmer for 45 minutes until the slices are tender. Drain. Make up the vinegar mixture as above, add the cooked orange slices, and simmer for 10 minutes or until the orange rind becomes transparent. Lift out the oranges with a slotted spoon and pack into sterilized, dry jars. Boil the syrup and finish as above.

spiced pickled beets

Makes **about six ½-pint jars**
Preparation time **25 minutes**
Cooking time **33–63 minutes**
(not including canning time)

10 **beets** (about 2 lb), leaves
  trimmed to about ¾ inch from
  the tops
2½ cup **distilled malt vinegar**
⅔ cup **granulated sugar**
1½-inch piece of **ginger root**,
  peeled and finely chopped
4 teaspoons **allspice berries**,
  coarsely crushed
½ teaspoon **black
  peppercorns**,
  coarsely crushed
½ teaspoon **salt**

Cook the beets in a saucepan of boiling water for
30–60 minutes, depending on their size, or until a knife
can be inserted into the largest one easily. Drain, let
cool, then peel off the skins with a small knife.

Meanwhile, prepare a boiling-water canner (see
pages 16–17) and heat the cleaned jars and lids
in simmering water. Set the screw bands aside.

Pour the vinegar into a saucepan, and add the sugar
and remaining ingredients. Heat gently, stirring
occasionally, until the sugar has dissolved. Increase
the heat and simmer for 3 minutes, then remove
from the heat and let cool.

Cut the beets into chunks and pack into the warmed
jars, working with one at a time. Pour the cold vinegar
mixture over the beets, covering them completely,
leaving a ½-inch headspace. Using a plastic spatula,
disperse any air bubbles, then clean the rim and threads
of the jars before covering with lids and securing with
screw bands. Repeat with the remaining jars.

Process the filled jars in a boiling-water canner for
30 minutes at sea level (see page 16). Let cool, clean
the jars, and label before storing.

To serve, try tossing some mixed lettuce leaves in a
crème fraîche dressing, topped with flaked mackerel.

For chile beets, follow the recipe as above, but omit
the ginger from the spiced vinegar mixture and add
1 teaspoon dried red pepper flakes and 3 star anise
instead. Continue as above.

pickled shallots

Makes **about one 1-pint jar**
Preparation time **30 minutes,**
   plus soaking and standing
Cooking time **5 minutes**
(not including canning time)

5 cups **small shallots,**
   pickling onions, or **pearl**
   onions
2 tablespoons **salt**
2 cups **sherry vinegar**
⅔ cup **superfine sugar**
½ cup firmly packed **light**
   brown sugar
2 **garlic cloves,** unpeeled
4 small **bay leaves**
4 sprigs **thyme**
4 sprigs **rosemary**
pinch of salt
½ teaspoon **peppercorns,**
   coarsely crushed

Trim a little off the tops and roots of the shallots, then put into a bowl and cover with boiling water. Let soak for 3 minutes, then pour off the water and cover again with cold water. Lift the shallots out one at a time and peel off the brown skins. Drain and layer in a bowl with the salt. Let stand overnight.

Meanwhile, prepare a boiling-water canner (see pages 16–17) and heat the cleaned jars and lids in simmering water. Set the screw bands aside.

Transfer the shallots to a colander and drain off as much liquid as possible. Rinse with cold water, drain, and dry with a kitchen towel.

Add the vinegar and sugar to a saucepan with the garlic, half the herbs, a pinch of salt, and peppercorns. Heat gently until the sugar dissolves, stirring occasionally. Increase the heat to medium and simmer for 5 minutes. Let cool.

Pack the shallots with the remaining herbs into the warmed jars. Strain and pour the cold vinegar syrup over the shallots, making sure they are covered with the vinegar and leaving a ½-inch headspace. Using a plastic spatula, disperse any air bubbles, then clean the rim and threads of the jars before covering with lids and securing with screw bands.

Process the filled jars in a boiling-water canner for 10 minutes at sea level (see page 16). Let cool, clean the jars, and label before storing.

For chile pickled shallots, omit the thyme and rosemary and add 1½ teaspoons dried red pepper flakes instead. Continue as above.

torshi

Makes **about six ½-pint jars**
Preparation time **30 minutes,
  plus soaking and standing**
Cooking time **2 minutes**
(not including canning time)

2 cups sliced **zucchini**
2 cups sliced **carrots**
1½ cups halved **green beans**
1 **fennel bulb**, sliced
1 **cauliflower**, cut into small
  florets
2 cups peeled **small pickling
  onions**
½ cup **salt**
5 cups **distilled malt vinegar**
  or **white wine vinegar**
1¼ cups **granulated sugar**
2 teaspoons **caraway seeds**
2 teaspoons **coriander seeds**,
  coarsely crushed
½ teaspoon **peppercorns**,
  coarsely crushed
6 small **dried red chiles**
6 **garlic cloves**, peeled and
  halved
4 stems **dill** or **fennel**

Layer the vegetables in a bowl with the salt, cover with a plate, and weigh down, then let soak overnight.

Pour the vinegar into a saucepan and add the sugar, caraway seeds, coriander seeds, and peppercorns, then the dried chiles, garlic, and 3 stems of dill or fennel. Bring to a boil, stirring until the sugar has dissolved, then set aside for the flavors to mingle.

Prepare a boiling-water canner (see pages 16–17) the next day, and heat the cleaned jars and lids in simmering water. Set the screw bands aside. Drain off the liquid from the vegetables, rinse with cold water, drain well, then pat dry with paper towel.

Pack into the warmed jars with the halved garlic and chiles from the vinegar mixture and the remaining fresh dill or fennel. Discard the cooked herbs from the spiced vinegar, then pour the cold vinegar mixture into the jars, leaving a ½-inch headspace. Using a plastic spatula, disperse any air bubbles, then clean the rim and threads of the jars before covering with lids and securing with screw bands.

Process the filled jars in a boiling-water canner for 15 minutes at sea level (see page 16). Let cool, clean the jars, and label before storing.

For pickled red cabbage, add 1 finely shredded medium red cabbage in place of the carrot, cauliflower, beans, and onions, then salt and let stand overnight as above. Drain off the liquid, then pack into warmed, dry jars and pour over the cold, flavored vinegar as above.

three-bean mustard pickle

Makes **about eight**
 ½-pint jars
Preparation time **25 minutes**
Cooking time **23 minutes**
(not including canning time)

1½ cups shelled **fava beans**
2½ cups **green bean** pieces
 (cut into thirds)
2½ cups thinly sliced
 wax beans
2 cups **cider vinegar** or **white
 wine vinegar**
2 cups **superfine sugar**
2 **medium onions**, chopped
3 **garlic cloves**, finely
 chopped
2 tablespoons **cornstarch**
1 tablespoon **turmeric**
1 tablespoon **mustard
 powder**
1 tablespoon **whole-grain
 mustard**
2 teaspoons **fennel seeds**,
 coarsely crushed
1 teaspoon **salt**
pepper
2 tablespoons **water**

Prepare a boiling-water canner (see pages 16–17) and heat the cleaned jars and lids in simmering water. Set the screw bands aside.

Bring a large saucepan of water to a boil, add the beans, cover, and bring back to a boil, then cook for 3 minutes. Drain and refresh with cold water, then drain again.

Pour the vinegar and sugar into a large saucepan, add the onions and garlic, then cover and bring to a boil. Reduce the heat and simmer for 10 minutes.

Mix together the remaining dry ingredients in a bowl, then mix to a smooth paste with the measured water. Stir into the vinegar mixture and cook, uncovered, for 5 minutes, stirring until thickened slightly. Add the blanched vegetables, cook for another 5 minutes, stirring, until the vegetables are just tender.

Ladle into warmed, dry jars, pressing the vegetables down below the liquid and leaving a ½-inch headspace. Using a plastic spatula, disperse any air bubbles, then clean the rim and threads of the jars before covering with lids and securing with screw bands.

Process the filled jars in a boiling-water canner for 15 minutes at sea level (see page 16). Let cool, clean the jars, and label before storing.

For curried bean pickle, use distilled malt vinegar instead of the wine vinegar or cider vinegar, and add 2 tablespoons mild curry powder in place of the mustard powder and whole-grain mustard. Continue as above.

piccalilli

Makes **about two to three ½-pint jars**
Preparation time **10 minutes, plus standing**
Cooking time **25 minutes** (not including canning time)

1 small **cauliflower**, broken into small florets, large stalks discarded
½ **cucumber**, peeled and coarsely chopped
2 **onions**, chopped
2 large **carrots**, peeled and cut into chunks
about ¼ cup **salt**
2 tablespoons **all-purpose flour**
1¼ cups **cider vinegar**
1¼ cups **granulated sugar**
½ teaspoon **ground turmeric**
½ teaspoon **ground ginger**
2 teaspoons **mustard powder**
pepper

Layer the vegetables in a large bowl, sprinkling each layer with salt, then cover and let stand overnight. The next day, lightly rinse and thoroughly dry them.

Prepare a boiling-water canner (see pages 16–17) and heat the cleaned jars and lids in simmering water. Set the screw bands aside.

Mix the flour to a smooth paste with a little of the vinegar. Heat the remaining vinegar in a large saucepan with the sugar, spices, and mustard powder over low heat, stirring continuously, until the sugar has dissolved. Increase the heat and bring to a boil, then season with pepper and add the vegetables. Bring back to a boil, reduce the heat, and simmer, uncovered, for 10 minutes. Remove the pan from the heat and gradually stir in the flour mixture. Return to the heat, bring to a boil and simmer for 5 minutes.

Ladle into warmed, dry jars, pressing the vegetables down below the liquid and leaving a ½-inch headspace. Using a plastic spatula, disperse any air bubbles, then clean the rim and threads of the jars before covering with lids and securing with screw bands.

Process the filled jars in a boiling-water canner for 15 minutes at sea level (see page 16). Let cool, clean the jars, and label before storing. Let mature for at least 3 weeks before using.

To serve, partner with slivers of Parma ham.

For Caribbean vegetable pickle, use 1 large eggplant cut into cubes, ½ small butternut squash, seeded, peeled, and cubed, ½ cauliflower, cut into florets, and 1 cup green bean pieces. Mix with 1 chopped onion, then layer with ¼ cup salt, soak, and continue as above.

honey pickled chiles

Makes **about two 1-pint jars**
Preparation time **15 minutes**
Cooking time **7–8 minutes**
(not including canning time)

1 lb whole **red cayenne chiles**
2 cups **cider vinegar** or
   white wine vinegar
¼ cup **honey**
¼ cup firmly packed **light
   brown sugar**
4 **bay leaves**
4 **sprigs thyme**
4 **garlic cloves**, peeled
   and sliced
1-inch piece **ginger root**,
   peeled and finely chopped
1 teaspoon **coriander seeds**
1 teaspoon **salt**

Prepare a boiling-water canner (see pages 16–17) and heat the cleaned jars and lids in simmering water. Set the screw bands aside.

Add the chiles to a saucepan of boiling water and cook for 2–3 minutes, until just softened. Transfer to a colander, rinse with cold water, and drain well.

Pour the vinegar into the drained pan and add all the remaining ingredients. Heat gently until the sugar has dissolved, then cook over medium heat for 5 minutes.

Pack the chiles and herbs from the vinegar tightly into the warmed, dry jars, then pour over the hot vinegar mixture, making sure that the chiles are completely covered by the vinegar and leaving a ½-inch headspace. Using a plastic spatula, disperse any air bubbles, then clean the rim and threads of the jars before covering with lids and securing with screw bands.

Process the filled jars in a boiling-water canner for 15 minutes at sea level (see page 16). Let cool, clean the jars, and label before storing. Let mature for at least 3–4 weeks before using.

For pickled baby peppers, omit the chiles and blanch 1 lb mixed baby red, yellow, and orange bell peppers in the same way as the chiles, then continue as above.

japanese pickled ginger

Makes **about two ½-pint jars**
Preparation time **15 minutes,
  plus standing**
Cooking time **3–4 minutes**

1 lb **ginger root**, peeled and
  very thinly sliced
¼ cup **salt**
1 cup **rice vinegar**
½ cup **granulated sugar**
2 **Thai green** or **red chiles**,
  sliced
10 **white peppercorns**

Sterilize the jars and lids, setting the screw bands aside.

Layer the ginger and salt in a bowl, cover with a plate, weigh down, and let stand overnight.

Transfer the ginger to a colander and drain off as much liquid as possible. Rinse with cold water, drain, and dry with paper towel.

Add the vinegar, sugar, chile slices, and peppercorns to a saucepan, heat gently until the sugar has dissolved, then bring to a boil and cook over medium heat for 2–3 minutes. Add the ginger and cook for 1 minute.

Pack the ginger and hot syrup into sterilized, dry jars, pressing the ginger below the vinegar mixture so that it is completely covered. Let cool, cover with the lids, label, and let mature stored in the refrigerator for about 3 weeks before using.

To serve, use as an accompaniment for sushi.

For pickled garlic, separate 4 garlic bulbs into cloves, then peel and cut each clove in half. Continue as above, omitting the ginger.

festive fruit preserves

mincemeat

Makes **about six 1-pint jars**
Preparation time
  20–30 minutes,
  plus standing
(not including canning time)

3½ cups chopped **currants**
3½ cups chopped **golden**
  raisins
3½ cups chopped **seedless**
  raisins
3 cups **chopped candied**
  peel
1¼ cups **blanched almonds**,
  finely chopped
3 **cooking apples**, peeled,
  cored, and coarsely grated
2¼ cups firmly packed **dark**
  brown sugar
1¼ cups **shredded suet** or
  1¾ sticks **butter**
1 teaspoon **ground** or **grated**
  nutmeg
1 teaspoon **ground cinnamon**
1 teaspoon **ground allspice**
grated rind of 2 **lemons**
juice of 1 **lemon**
2–4 tablespoons **brandy**

Put the currants, golden raisins, raisins, candied peel, and almonds into a large bowl. Add the apples, sugar, suet (or butter), spices, and lemon rind and juice and stir to mix thoroughly. Cover the bowl with plastic wrap and let the mincemeat stand for 2 days.

Prepare a boiling-water canner (see pages 16–17) and heat the cleaned jars and lids in simmering water. Set the screw bands aside.

Stir the mincemeat thoroughly, then add the brandy.

Pack into the warmed jars, working with one at a time. Fill each jar to ½ inch from the top. Using a plastic spatula, disperse any air bubbles, then clean the rim and threads of the jar before covering with a lid and securing with a screw band. Repeat with the remaining jars.

Process the filled jars in a boiling-water canner for 30 minutes at sea level (see page 16). Let cool, clean the jars, and label. Store for at least 2 weeks before using.

For cranberry mincemeat, use 2¾ cups each of currants, golden raisins, and seedless raisins and 2 cups dried cranberries. Continue as above.

apricot & ginger mincemeat

Makes **about four 1-pint jars**
Preparation time **30 minutes,
  plus standing**
(not including canning time)

²/₃ cup finely chopped
  crystallized ginger
2 cups finely chopped **dried
  apricots**
1¾ cups finely chopped
  raisins
1¼ cups finely chopped
  golden raisins
1¼ cups **dried currants**
¼ cup **chopped candied peel**
½ cup chopped **blanched
  almonds**
1½ **cooking apples**, peeled,
  cored, and grated
juice and grated rind of
  3 **oranges**
juice and grated rind of
  2 **lemons**
1 cup plus 2 tablespoons
  firmly packed **light brown
  sugar**
3½ cups grated **carrots**
¼ teaspoon **grated nutmeg**
½ teaspoon **ground allspice**
²/₃ cup **brandy**
¼ cup **rum**

Put the ginger, apricots, raisins, and golden raisins into a large bowl with the currants, candied peel, and almonds.

Add the apples to a separate bowl and mix in the orange and lemon rinds and juices, then stir into the chopped fruit with the sugar.

Add the carrots to the bowl, along with the spices, brandy, and rum, then cover the bowl with plastic wrap and let the mincemeat stand for 2 days, stirring frequently.

Prepare a boiling-water canner (see pages 16–17) and heat the cleaned jars and lids in simmering water. Set the screw bands aside.

Pack into the warmed jars, working with one at a time. Fill each jar to ½ inch from the top. Using a plastic spatula, disperse any air bubbles, then clean the rim and threads of the jar before covering with a lid and securing with a screw band. Repeat with the remaining jars.

Process the filled jars in a boiling-water canner for 30 minutes at sea level (see page 16). Let cool, clean the jars, and label. Store for at least 3–4 weeks before using.

To serve, use as a filling for mincemeat pies.

For mulled wine cherry mincemeat, mix 1 cup dried cherries with 1 cup chopped dried apricots, then add to the dried vine fruits, candied peel, almonds, apples, citrus rinds and juice, and spices as above. Stir in ²/₃ cup port and ¼ cup brandy and continue as above.

cranberry mincemeat with port

Makes **about four ½-pint jars**
Preparation time **20 minutes,**
 plus standing
Cooking time **5 minutes**
(not including canning time)

2 cups **cranberries**
1 large **cooking apple,**
 peeled, cored, and diced
3 tablespoons **water**
3 cups **mixed dried fruit**
1 teaspoon **ground cinnamon**
½ teaspoon **freshly grated**
 nutmeg
¼ teaspoon **ground clove**
1 cup firmly packed **light**
 brown sugar
⅔ cup **shredded vegetable**
 suet or **butter**
grated rind of 1 **orange**
½ cup **ruby port**

Put the cranberries and apple into a saucepan with the measured water and cook, uncovered, for 5 minutes, stirring occasionally, until the fruits are softened but still holding their shape. Let cool in the pan.

Add the dried fruit to a large bowl and mix in the remaining ingredients. Stir in the cooked fruit, then cover the bowl with plastic wrap and let stand overnight.

Prepare a boiling-water canner (see pages 16–17) and heat the cleaned jars and lids in simmering water. Set the screw bands aside.

Stir the mincemeat mixture, then pack into the warmed jars, working with one at a time. Fill each jar to ½ inch from the top. Using a plastic spatula, disperse any air bubbles, then clean the rim and threads of the jar before covering with a lid and securing with a screw band. Repeat with the remaining jars.

Process the filled jars in a boiling-water canner for 30 minutes at sea level (see page 16). Let cool, clean the jars, and label. Store for 3–4 weeks before using.

To serve, use as a filling for mincemeat pies.

For prune & whiskey mincemeat, add 2 cups pitted and diced prunes to a saucepan with the apple and water as above. Add the dried fruits and continue adding the spices, sugar, suet (or butter), orange rind, and ½ cup whiskey.

figs in vanilla syrup

Makes **about one 1-pint jar**
Preparation time **20 minutes**
Cooking time **about
45 minutes**

8–9 firm **fresh figs**, halved and
blanched in boiling water for
2 minutes
½ cup **superfine sugar**
1 cup **water**
½ **vanilla bean**, slit lengthwise
½ teaspoon **citric acid**

Prepare a boiling-water canner (see pages 16–17) and heat the cleaned jar and lid in simmering water. Set the screw band aside.

Pack the figs into the warm jar with the cut sides facing out. Pack the center of the jar tightly and put two halves, cut-side up, in the top of the jar.

Put the sugar, measured water, and vanilla bean into a saucepan. Slowly bring to a boil and heat, stirring continuously, until the sugar has completely dissolved. Boil for 1 minute, then remove from the heat.

Lift the vanilla bean out of the syrup and, using a small knife, scrape out the black seeds into the syrup and stir in the citric acid. Tuck the vanilla bean down the side of the jar.

Pour the syrup over the figs to cover completely, leaving a ½-inch headspace, and adding boiling water, if needed. Using a plastic spatula, disperse any air bubbles, then clean the rim and threads of the jar before covering with a lid and securing with a screw band.

Process the filled jar in a boiling-water canner for 45 minutes at sea level (see page 16). Let cool, clean the jar, and label before storing.

For apricots in marsala syrup, halve 8–9 fresh apricots and pack tightly into a jar, without blanching. Make the syrup as above with ⅔ cup sugar and 1 cup water. Remove from the heat and stir in marsala wine and ½ teaspoon citric acid. Pour the syrup over the apricots and continue as above, but processing in the water bath for 25 minutes.

blueberries in kirsch

Makes **about one 1-pint jar**
Preparation time **10 minutes,
    plus standing**

1 ¼ cups **blueberries**, stems
    removed
¼ cup **superfine sugar**
½ cup **kirsch**

Sterilize the jars and lid, setting the screw band aside.

Pick over the blueberries, discarding any very soft
ones. Prick each berry with a fork, then layer in the
sterilized, dry jar, sprinkling each layer with some sugar.

Pour the kirsch over the berries. Seal tightly and shake
once or twice.

Let mature in the refrigerator, turning the jar
upside down every day for 4 days, until the sugar
has completely dissolved. Label and store in the
refrigerator for 3–4 weeks before using.

To serve, drizzle over pancakes served with vanilla
ice cream.

For cherries in brandy, omit the blueberries and use
1 ¼ cups small, firm cherries that have had their stems
removed. Prick the cherries and layer in the jar with
the sugar, then top up with brandy in place of kirsch.
Continue as above.

herbed pickled plums

Makes **about three 1-pint jars**
Preparation time **20 minutes**
Cooking time **3 minutes**
(not including canning time)

3 cups **white
  wine vinegar**
2½ cups **superfine sugar**
7 **rosemary sprigs**
7 **thyme sprigs**
7 small **bay leaves**
4 **lavender sprigs** (optional)
4 **garlic cloves**, unpeeled
1 teaspoon **salt**
½ teaspoon **multicolored
  peppercorns**
1½ quarts firm **red plums**
  (about 3 lb), washed
  and pricked

Prepare a boiling-water canner (see pages 16–17) and heat the cleaned jars and lids in simmering water. Set the screw bands aside.

Pour the vinegar and sugar into a medium saucepan, add 4 each of the rosemary and thyme sprigs and bay leaves, all the lavender, if using, and the garlic, salt, and peppercorns. Cook gently, stirring once or twice, until the sugar has dissolved. Bring to a boil, then boil for 3 minutes, until the mixture becomes syrupy.

Pack the plums into the warmed jars, working with one at a time, and tuck the remaining fresh herbs into them. Strain the hot vinegar into the jars, leaving a ½ inch headspace. Using a plastic spatula, disperse any air bubbles, then clean the rim and threads of the jar before covering with a lid and securing with a screw band. Repeat with the remaining jars.

Process the filled jars in a boiling-water canner for 10 minutes at sea level (see page 16). Let cool, clean the jars, and label. Store for 3–4 weeks before using. The plums will lose color slightly.

For pickled red bell peppers, cut the tops off 4 red bell peppers and scoop out the core and seeds. Add to a saucepan of boiling water and cook for 3 minutes, until just softened. Drain well, then dry on a kitchen towel. Heat 2½ cups distilled malt vinegar with 1¼ cups granulated sugar until the sugar has dissolved, then cover and simmer for 10 minutes. Pack the peppers and liquid in the jars as above, and process in the water bath for 15 minutes.

orange & whiskey marmalade

Makes **about four ½-pint jars**
Preparation time **30 minutes**
Cooking time **1 hour**
   30 minutes–1 hour
   35 minutes
(not including canning time)

6 **Seville or bitter oranges**
   (about 2 lb)
juice of **1 lemon**
5 cups **granulated sugar,**
   warmed
¼ cup **whiskey**

Prepare a boiling-water canner (see pages 16–17) and heat the cleaned jars and lids in simmering water. Set the screw bands aside.

Add the whole oranges to a large saucepan in a single layer. Just cover with cold water, bring to a boil, cover with a lid, and cook gently for 1 hour, or until the oranges can be pierced easily with a sharp knife. Let cool.

Remove the oranges from the pan with a slotted spoon, draining well. Reserve 3¾ cups of the cooking liquid. Halve the oranges, scoop out the seeds, and reserve. Cut the oranges into thin slices. Add the slices to the pan with the seeds tied in a square of cheesecloth, the measured cooking liquid, and the lemon juice. Simmer over medium heat for 10 minutes, until the orange slices are tender.

Add the sugar and heat gently, stirring occasionally, until the sugar has dissolved. Bring to a boil, then boil rapidly until setting point is reached (20–25 minutes). Lift out the cheesecloth bag, squeezing well. Stir in the whiskey and let cool for 10 minutes. Ladle into the warmed jars, working with one at a time. Fill each jar to ¼ inch from the top. Using a plastic spatula, disperse any air bubbles. Clean the rim and threads of the jar, cover with a lid, and secure with a screw band. Repeat with the remaining jars.

Process the filled jars in a boiling-water canner for 10 minutes at sea level (see page 16). Let cool, clean the jars, and label before storing.

For chunky orange marmalade, follow the recipe as above, but when measuring the water, add the juice of 2 lemons and omit the whiskey.

ginger marmalade

Makes **about five 1-pint jars**
Preparation time **30 minutes,
plus standing**
Cooking time **2¾ hours**
(not including canning time)

8 **lemons**
2 large **oranges**
10½ cups **water**
3-inch piece **ginger root,**
  sliced and finely shredded
7½ cups **granulated sugar**
1 tablespoon **butter** (optional)

Prepare a boiling-water canner (see pages 16–17) and heat the cleaned jars and lids in simmering water. Set the screw bands aside.

Pare the rind from the fruits with a vegetable peeler and cut into fine shreds. Halve the fruits and squeeze out the juice. Put the juice and rind into a saucepan with the measured water and ginger. Chop the fruit halves, including the pith, and tie in a square of cheesecloth. Add to the pan and bring to a boil. Reduce the heat, cover, and simmer for 2 hours, or until the ginger and rind are tender.

Remove the pan from the heat and let stand until cool enough to handle, then squeeze all the juices back into the marmalade and discard the bag. Add the sugar to the pan and cook over low heat, stirring continuously, until the sugar has dissolved. Increase the heat and bring to a boil, then boil hard to setting point (20–30 minutes). Skim with a skimming spoon or stir in butter, if needed.

Ladle into the warmed jars, working with one at a time. Fill each jar to ¼ inch from the top. Using a plastic spatula, disperse any air bubbles. Clean the rim and threads of the jar, cover with a lid, and secure with a screw band. Repeat with the remaining jars.

Process the filled jars in a boiling-water canner for 10 minutes at sea level (see page 16). Let cool, clean the jars, and label before storing.

For lime marmalade, cut 8 limes into quarters lengthwise, then into long, fine slices, removing all the seeds. Mix the fruit in a large saucepan. Add 6½ cups water, bring to a boil, then reduce the heat, cover, and simmer for 1½ hours. Add 7½ cups sugar and proceed as above.

winter fig & orange jam

Makes **about six 1-pint jars**
Preparation time **20 minutes**
Cooking time **45–50 minutes**
(not including canning time)

2½ cups **dried figs**
9 **cooking apples** (about 3 lb)
2 **oranges**
3¾ cups **water**
2 teaspoons **ground cinnamon**
6¼ cups **granulated sugar**

Prepare a boiling-water canner (see pages 16–17). Sterilize the jars and lids. Set the screw bands aside.

Chop the figs, then add to a large saucepan. Quarter, core, and peel the apples, then cut into small dice. Finely chop the whole oranges—or coarsely chop, then process in a food processor until finely chopped. Add to the pan with the measured water and cinnamon. Cover and cook gently for 30 minutes, stirring occasionally, until the fruit is soft.

Add the sugar and heat gently, stirring occasionally, until the sugar has dissolved. Bring to a boil, then boil rapidly for 15–20 minutes, until thick. This jam has more of a chutneylike consistency, so stir more frequently the thicker it becomes so that it doesn't stick to the bottom of the pan.

Ladle into the warmed jars, working with one at a time. Fill each jar to ¼ inch from the top. Using a plastic spatula, disperse any air bubbles. Clean the rim and threads of the jar, cover with a lid, and secure with a screw band. Repeat with the remaining jars.

Process the filled jars in a boiling-water canner for 5 minutes at sea level (see page 16). Let cool, clean the jars, and label before storing.

For winter apricot & orange jam, follow the recipe as above, but use 4 cups diced dried apricots instead of the figs.

apricot & cointreau curd

Makes **2 jars**
Preparation time **25 minutes**
Cooking time **55 minutes–**
  1 hour 5 minutes

1 cup diced **dried apricots**
⅔ cup **water**
juice of 2 **lemons**
1 stick **butter**, diced
2 cups **superfine sugar**
4 **eggs**, beaten
3 tablespoons **Cointreau**
  or **Grand Marnier**

Sterilize the jars and lids.

Add the apricots and measured water to a saucepan, then cover and cook gently for about 15 minutes, until soft. Let cool for 10–15 minutes.

Puree the apricots in a food processor or blender with the lemon juice. Melt the butter in a large bowl set over a saucepan of simmering water. Add the apricot puree and sugar, then strain in the eggs and mix together. Cook for 40–50 minutes, stirring occasionally, until the sugar has dissolved and the mixture has thickened.

Stir in the liqueur, then ladle into sterilized, dry jars, let cool, cover, and store in the refrigerator for up to 1 week.

To serve, this curd mingles perfectly with lightly whipped cream and crumbled meringues, for an easy dessert.

For apricot & orange curd, cook the apricots in ⅔ cup orange juice. Continue as above, but omit the liqueur.

black currant & mulled wine jelly

Makes **about four 1-pint jars**

Preparation time **30 minutes, plus straining**

Cooking time **55 minutes– 1 hour**

(not including canning time)

12 cups fresh or frozen **black currants** (about 3 lb)

3 cups **water**

2 cups **red wine**

4-inch **cinnamon stick,** broken into pieces

1 teaspoon **whole cloves**

rind of 1 **orange**

rind of 1 **lemon**

about 6¼ cups **granulated sugar**

1 tablespoon **butter** (optional)

Prepare a boiling-water canner (see pages 16–17). Sterilize the jars and lids. Set the screw bands aside.

Add the black currants, measured water, and wine to a large saucepan, then add the spices and fruit rinds. Bring to a boil, then cover and simmer gently for 40 minutes, stirring and mashing the fruit occasionally with a fork, until soft. Let cool slightly, then pour into a scalded jelly bag suspended over a large bowl and let drip for several hours.

Measure the clear liquid and then pour back into a saucepan. Add 2½ cups sugar for every 2½ cups liquid to the pan. Heat gently, stirring occasionally, until the sugar has dissolved.

Bring to a boil, then boil rapidly until setting point is reached (15–20 minutes). Skim with a skimming spoon or stir in butter, if needed.

Ladle into the sterilized jars, working with one at a time. Fill each jar to ¼ inch from the top. Clean the rim and threads of the jar before covering with a lid and securing with a screw band. Repeat with the remaining jars.

Process the filled jars in a boiling-water canner for 5 minutes at sea level (see page 16). Let cool, clean the jars, and label before storing.

To serve, this jelly can be spooned on top of cupcakes that have been decorated with piped buttercream.

For cranberry mulled wine jelly, make up the jelly with 12 cups cranberries (about 3 lb) instead of the black currants. Continue as above.

cranberry & red wine chutney

Makes **about three ½-pint jars**
Preparation time **30 minutes**
Cooking time **1¼–1½ hours**
(not including canning time)

4 cups **fresh** or **frozen**
   cranberries (if frozen, there
   is no need to defrost first)
2 **red onions**, thinly sliced
1½ cups **mixed dried fruit**
1¼ cups firmly packed **light**
   brown sugar
⅔ cup **red wine**
⅔ cup **red wine vinegar**
2 teaspoons **ground allspice**
1 teaspoon **dried red pepper**
   flakes
1 teaspoon **salt**
½ teaspoon **pepper**

Prepare a boiling-water canner (see pages 16–17) and heat the cleaned jars and lids in simmering water. Set the screw bands aside.

Add all the ingredients to a medium saucepan, cover, and simmer gently for 1 hour, stirring occasionally, until softened.

Remove the lid and cook for 15–30 minutes, until thick, stirring more frequently toward the end of cooking, until the cranberries are soft and the chutney is thick.

Ladle into the sterilized jars, working with one at a time. Fill each jar to ¼ inch from the top. Clean the rim and threads of the jar before covering with a lid and securing with a screw band. Repeat with the remaining jars.

Process the filled jars in a boiling-water canner for 10 minutes at sea level (see page 16). Let cool, clean the jars, and label before storing.

To serve, this chutney goes perfectly with cold sliced turkey, watercress, and cherry tomatoes.

For Christmas plum chutney, omit the cranberries and add 10 pitted and sliced plums instead, and 1¼ cups red wine vinegar instead of the vinegar and red wine. Continue as above, but process in the water bath for 15 minutes.

index

**ale, apple, & mustard
   chutney** 142
almonds
   chunky fig, almond, &
      orange marmalade 118
   green grape & almond
      conserve 60
Andrew's plums 164
apple & tomato relish 174
apples
   ale, apple, & mustard
      chutney 142
   apple, apricot, &
      elderflower butter 68
   apple & blackberry jam 32
   apple & ginger beer
      chutney 142
   apple & ginger curd 80
   apple & ginger wine
      butter 74
   apple & orange
      marmalade 118
   apple & tomato
      chutney 144
   apple & tomato relish 174
   apple, prune, & vanilla
      butter 68
   apple, zucchini, & ginger
      preserves 36
   beet & apple relish 178
   blackberry & apple
      paste 90
   blackberry, apple, &
      cinnamon jam 24
   crab apple jelly 112
   cranberry & apple
      preserves 24
   elderberry & apple
      jelly 104
   green tomato
      chutney 148
   minted blackberry &
      apple jelly 106
   mulberry & apple
      jelly 110
   orchard fruit preserves 32

quince, apple, &
   cinnamon jelly 106
reduced-sugar apricot,
   date, & apple
   preserves 58
rosehip & apple jelly 104
sour apple & rosemary
   jelly 96
spiced apple butter 74
spiced apple curd 80
windfall apple & cider
   jelly 98
windfall apple & ginger
   jelly 98
apricots
   apple, apricot, &
      elderflower butter 68
   apricot & Cointreau
      curd 228
   apricot & ginger
      mincemeat 212
   apricot & orange
      curd 228
   apricot & vodka
      preserves 48
   apricot, orange,
      & cardamom
      marmalade 120
   apricot, orange, & ginger
      marmalade 120
   apricots in marsala
      syrup 216
   reduced-sugar apricot
      preserves 58
   reduced-sugar apricot,
      date, & apple
      preserves 58
   winter apricot & orange
      jam 226
autumnal harvest
   chutney 144

bananas
banana & chocolate
   jam 64
banana & date
   preserves 64
beans
   Caribbean vegetable
      pickle 202

curried bean pickle 200
green bean chutney 146
three-bean mustard
   pickle 200
zucchini & mixed bean
   chutney 146
beets
   beet & apple relish 178
   beet & horseradish
      relish 178
   chile beets 194
   spiced pickled
      beets 194
bell peppers
   cucumber & bell pepper
      relish 176
   mixed bell pepper
      relish 176
   pickled baby peppers 204
   pickled red bell
      peppers 220
   pumpkin & red bell
      pepper chutney 152
   ratatouille chutney 138
   roasted root
      chutney 152
   South Seas relish 172
   tomato & bell pepper
      relish 182
berries
   quick mixed berry
      preserves 54
   frozen berry preserves 62
   mixed berry preserves 62
bitter lemon & lime jelly 102
bitter lime & Pernod
   jelly 102
blackberries
   apple & blackberry
      preserves 32
   blackberry & apple
      paste 90
   blackberry, apple, &
      cinnamon preserves 24
   elderberry & blackberry
      jam 28
   fresh fig & blackberry
      preserves 30
   gingered blackberry &
      fig preserves 30

minted blackberry &
   apple jelly 106
plum & zucchini
   preserves 36
black currant & mulled
   wine jelly 230
black & red currant
   jam 28
bloody mary jelly 100
blueberries
   blueberries in kirsch 218
   blueberry & honey jam 26
   blueberry & raspberry
      preserves 42
brandy
   cherries in brandy 218
boiling-water canners
   16–17
butternut squash
   Caribbean vegetable
      pickle 202
butters *see* fruit butters

cabbage
   pickled red cabbage
      198
candy thermometers 10
canning 16–17
cardamom
   apricot, orange,
      & cardamom
      marmalade 120
   gooseberry relish with
      cardamom 170
Caribbean vegetable
   pickle 202
carrots
   carrot & cilantro
      chutney 160
   piccalilli 202
   torshi 198
cauliflower
   Caribbean vegetable
      pickle 202
   piccalilli 202
   torshi 198
champagne
   strawberry champagne
      preserves 46
cheesecloth 11

cherries
  cherries in brandy 218
  cherry & raspberry
    preserves 42
  mulled wine cherry
    mincemeat 212
chestnuts
  chestnut, cinnamon, &
    orange jam 44
  chestnut jam with
    whiskey 44
  chestnut, onion, &
    fennel chutney 156
chiles
  chile & red tomato
    relish 168
  chile beets 194
  chile pickled shallots
    196
  chile tomato jelly 100
  eggplant & chile
    chutney 140
  honey pickled chiles 204
  hot chile & tamarind
    chutney 154
  hot corn relish 180
  pickled lemons with
    chile & garlic 188
  South Seas relish 172
  sweet chile & kaffir lime
    relish 172
chocolate
  banana & chocolate
    jam 64
Christmas plum
  chutney 232
chunky fig, almond, &
  orange marmalade 118
chunky orange
  marmalade 222
chutneys 8
  ale, apple, & mustard
    chutney 142
  Andrew's plums 164
  apple & ginger beer
    chutney 142
  apple & tomato
    chutney 144
  autumnal harvest
    chutney 144

carrot & cilantro
  chutney 160
cayenne pepper &
  garlic chutney 154
chestnut, onion, &
  fennel chutney 156
Christmas plum
  chutney 232
cranberry & red wine
  chutney 232
eggplant & chile
  chutney 140
eggplant & mint
  chutney 140
garlicky Mediterranean
  chutney 138
gingered parsnip &
  cilantro chutney 160
green bean chutney 146
green tomato & mango
  chutney 148
green tomato
  chutney 148
hot chile & tamarind
  chutney 154
mango & black onion
  seed chutney 136
mango & pineapple
  chutney 136
peach & date
  chutney 158
peach & orange
  chutney 158
pumpkin & date
  chutney 150
pumpkin & red bell
  pepper chutney 152
pumpkin & walnut
  chutney 150
ratatouille chutney 138
red onion & raisin
  chutney 156
roasted root chutney 152
smooth plum & tomato
  chutney 164
storage 17
sweet potato & orange
  chutney 162
sweet potato, ginger, &
  orange chutney 162

zucchini & mixed bean
  chutney 146
cider
  windfall apple & cider
    jelly 98
cilantro
  carrot & cilantro
    chutney 160
  gingered parsnip &
    coriander cilantro 160
cinnamon
  blackberry, apple, &
    cinnamon preserves 24
  chestnut, cinnamon, &
    orange jam 44
  cranberry & cinnamon
    butter 72
  quince, apple, &
    cinnamon jelly 106
citric acid 12
cloves
  plum & clove paste 88
coconut
  lime & coconut curd 84
Cointreau
  apricot & Cointreau
    curd 228
colorful corn relish 180
conserves 8
  green grape & almond
    conserve 60
corn
  colorful corn relish 180
  hot corn relish 180
crab apple jelly 112
cranberries
  cranberry & apple
    preserves 24
  cranberry & cinnamon
    butter 72
  cranberry & pear
    butter 72
  cranberry & red wine
    chutney 232
  cranberry mincemeat
    210
  cranberry mincemeat
    with port 214
  cranberry mulled wine
    jelly 230

cucumber
  cucumber & bell pepper
    relish 176
  piccalilli 202
  sweet pickled
    cucumbers 192
curds see fruit curds
cutting boards 11

**dark Oxford
  marmalade** 116
dates
  banana & date
    preserves 64
  peach & date
    chutney 158
  pumpkin & date
    chutney 150
  reduced-sugar apricot,
    date, & apple
    preserves 58

eggplants
  Caribbean vegetable
    pickle 202
  eggplant & chile
    chutney 140
  eggplant & mint
    chutney 140
  tomato & eggplant
    relish 182
elderberries
  elderberry & apple
    jelly 104
  elderberry & blackberry
    jam 28
elderflower syrup (cordial)
  apple, apricot, &
    elderflower butter 68
  gooseberry &
    elderflower curd 86
equipment 10

fava beans
  curried bean pickle 200
  three-bean mustard
    pickle 200
fennel
  chestnut, onion, &
    fennel chutney 156

torshi 198
figs
  chunky fig, almond, &
    orange marmalade 118
  figs in vanilla syrup 216
  fresh fig & blackberry
    preserves 30
  gingered blackberry &
    fig preserves 30
  winter fig & orange
    jam 226
frozen mixed berry
  preserves 62
fruit
  choosing 11–12
  pectin levels 12, 13
fruit butters 9
  apple & ginger wine
    butter 74
  apple, apricot, &
    elderflower butter 68
  apple, prune, & vanilla
    butter 68
  cranberry & cinnamon
    butter 72
  cranberry & pear
    butter 72
  pear & plum butter 70
  pear & strawberry
    butter 70
  pumpkin & brown sugar
    butter 76
  spiced apple butter 74
  spiced pumpkin
    butter 76
fruit curds 8, 9
  apple & ginger curd 80
  apricot & Cointreau
    curd 228
  apricot & orange
    curd 228
  gooseberry &
    elderflower curd 86
  gooseberry curd 86
  lemon curd 78
  lime & coconut curd 84
  lime & passion fruit
    curd 84
  raspberry & lemon
    curd 82

raspberry & red
  grapefruit curd 82
St. Clement's curd 78
spiced apple curd 80
fruit pastes 9
  blackberry & apple
    paste 90
  pear & red wine
    paste 88
  plum & clove paste 88
  quince paste 90
funnels 10–11

garlic
  cayenne pepper &
    garlic chutney 154
  garlicky Mediterranean
    chutney 138
  garlicky tomato
    relish 174
  hot chile & tamarind
    chutney 154
  pickled garlic 206
  pickled lemons with
    chile & garlic 188
  ratatouille chutney
    138
ginger
  apple & ginger curd 80
  apple, zucchini, & ginger
    preserves 36
  apricot & ginger
    mincemeat 212
  apricot, orange, & ginger
    marmalade 120
  ginger & lemon jelly
    marmalade 122
  ginger marmalade 224
  gingered blackberry &
    fig preserves 30
  gingered parsnip &
    cilantro chutney 160
  gingered pineapple &
    raisin preserves 34
  Japanese pickled
    ginger 206
  sweet potato, ginger, &
    orange chutney 162
  windfall apple & ginger
    jelly 98

ginger beer
  apple & ginger beer
    chutney 142
ginger wine
  apple & ginger wine
    butter 74
golden Oxford
  marmalade 116
gooseberries
  gooseberry &
    elderflower curd 86
  gooseberry & rosemary
    jelly 96
  gooseberry & strawberry
    preserves 38
  gooseberry curd 86
  gooseberry relish with
    cardamom 170
grapefruit
  grapefruit jelly
    marmalade 124
  mixed citrus
    marmalade 132
  raspberry & red
    grapefruit curd 82
  ruby orange
    marmalade 124
grapes
  grape & port jelly 112
  green grape & almond
    conserve 60
  green grape preserves 60
green beans
  curried bean pickle 200
  green bean chutney 146
  three-bean mustard
    pickle 200
  torshi 198
  zucchini & mixed bean
    chutney 146
green tomato & mango
  chutney 148
green tomato chutney 148
greengages
  spiced greengage
    preserves 22

herbed pickled plums 220
honey
  blueberry & honey jam 26

honey pickled chiles 204
raspberry & honey jam 26
horseradish
  beet & horseradish
    relish 178

jams 8
  banana & chocolate
    jam 64
  black & red currant
    jam 28
  blueberry & honey
    jam 26
  chestnut, cinnamon, &
    orange jam 44
  chestnut jam with
    whiskey 44
  elderberry & blackberry
    jam 28
  green grape & apricot
    jam 60
  making 12–16
    canning 16–17
    jars 16, 17
    problems 15–16
    reduced-sugar jams 17
    storage 17
    sugar for 14
    testing for setting
      14–15
  no-cook raspberry jam 56
  no-cook strawberry
    jam 56
  peach jam 52
  raspberry & honey jam 26
  strawberry & lavender
    jam 20
  strawberry jam 20
  winter apricot & orange
    jam 226
  winter fig & orange
    jam 226
Japanese pickled
  ginger 206
jars
  choosing 16
  lids for 16
jellies 8–9
  bitter lemon & lime
    jelly 102

bitter lime & Pernod
jelly 102
bloody mary jelly 100
chile tomato jelly 100
crab apple jelly 112
elderberry & apple
jelly 104
gooseberry & rosemary
jelly 96
grape & port jelly 112
making 12–16
canning 16–17
jars 17
minted blackberry &
apple jelly 106
mulberry & apple
jelly 110
plum & crushed
peppercorn jelly 94
plum & star anise
jelly 94
quince, apple, &
cinnamon jelly 106
red currant & lavender
jelly 108
red currant & orange
jelly 108
rosehip & apple
jelly 104
sour apple & rosemary
jelly 96
strawberry & rhubarb
jelly 110
windfall apple & cider
jelly 98
windfall apple & ginger
jelly 98
jelly bags 11
jerked tomato
relish 168

kirsch
blueberries in
kirsch 218
kiwis
pineapple & kiwi
preserves 50
knives 11
kumquats
pickled kumquats 190

ladles 11
lavender
red currant & lavender
jelly 108
strawberry & lavender
jam 20
lemon squeezers 11
lemons
apple & orange
marmalade 118
bitter lemon & lime
jelly 102
dark Oxford
marmalade 116
ginger & lemon jelly
marmalade 122
ginger marmalade 224
lemon & pear
marmalade 126
lemon & quince
marmalade 126
lemon curd 78
lime jelly marmalade
122
mixed citrus
marmalade 132
pickled lemons with
chile & garlic 188
preserved lemons 188
pressure cooker
marmalade 130
raspberry & lemon
curd 82
St. Clement's
curd 78
three-fruit shred
marmalade 132
limes
bitter lemon & lime
jelly 102
bitter lime & Pernod
jelly 102
lime & coconut
curd 84
lime & passion fruit
curd 84
lime jelly marmalade
122
lime marmalade 224
lime pickle 190

mixed citrus
marmalade 132
orange & lime
marmalade 130
papaya & lime
preserves 40
pineapple, mango, &
lime marmalade 128
St. Clement's curd 78
South Seas relish 172
sweet chile & kaffir lime
relish 172
three-fruit shred
marmalade 132
lychee & strawberry
preserves 46

mangoes
green tomato & mango
chutney 148
mango & passion fruit
preserves 40
mango & black onion
seed chutney 136
mango & pineapple
chutney 136
pineapple, mango, &
lime marmalade 128
marmalades 8, 9
apple & orange
marmalade 118
apricot, orange, &
cardamom
marmalade 120
apricot, orange, & ginger
marmalade 120
chunky fig, almond, &
orange marmalade
118
chunky orange
marmalade 222
dark Oxford
marmalade 116
ginger & lemon jelly
marmalade 122
ginger marmalade 224
golden Oxford
marmalade 116
grapefruit jelly
marmalade 124

lemon & pear
marmalade 126
lemon & quince
marmalade 126
lime jelly marmalade 122
lime marmalade 224
making 12–16
jars 17
mixed citrus
marmalade 132
orange & lime
marmalade 130
orange & whiskey
marmalade 222
pineapple, mango, &
lime marmalade 128
pineapple
marmalade 128
pressure cooker
marmalade 130
ruby orange
marmalade 124
three-fruit shred
marmalade 132
marsala
apricots in marsala
syrup 216
mason-style jar 16
mincemeat 9, 210–11
apricot & ginger
mincemeat 212
covering jars 17
cranberry mincemeat 210
cranberry mincemeat
with port 214
mulled wine cherry
mincemeat 212
prune & whiskey
mincemeat 214
mint
eggplant & mint
chutney 140
minted blackberry &
apple jelly 106
mixed berry
preserves 62
mold on jam 16
mulberry & apple jelly 110
mulled wine cherry
mincemeat 212

mustard
ale, apple, & mustard
chutney 142
three-bean mustard
pickle 200

**no-cook raspberry
jam** 56
no-cook strawberry
jam 56

onions
chestnut, onion, & fennel
chutney 156
piccalilli 202
red onion & raisin
chutney 156
oranges
apple & orange
marmalade 118
apricot & orange
curd 228
apricot, orange, &
cardamom
marmalade 120
apricot, orange, & ginger
marmalade 120
chestnut, cinnamon, &
orange jam 44
chunky fig, almond, &
orange marmalade 118
chunky orange
marmalade 222
cranberry, apple, &
orange jam 24
dark Oxford
marmalade 116
ginger marmalade 224
golden Oxford
marmalade 116
mixed citrus
marmalade 132
orange & lime
marmalade 130
orange & whiskey
marmalade 222
peach & orange
chutney 158
pressure cooker
marmalade 130

red currant & orange
jelly 108
ruby orange
marmalade 124
St. Clement's curd 78
sweet pickled
oranges 192
sweet potato & orange
chutney 162
sweet potato, ginger, &
orange chutney 162
three-fruit shred
marmalade 132
winter fig & orange
jam 226
orchard fruit preserves 32

**papaya & lime
preserves** 40
parsnips
gingered parsnip &
cilantro chutney 160
roasted root chutney
152
passion fruit
lime & passion fruit
curd 84
mango & passion fruit
preserves 40
pineapple & passion
fruit preserves 34
peaches
peach & date
chutney 158
peach & orange
chutney 158
peach & vanilla
preserves 48
peach jam 52
peach melba
preserves 52
pickled peach
dressing 186
pickled peaches 186
spiced peach relish 170
pears
cranberry & pear
butter 72
lemon & pear
marmalade 126

orchard fruit jam 32
pear & plum butter 70
pear & red wine
paste 88
pear & strawberry
butter 70
pectin 12–13
peppercorns
plum & crushed
peppercorn jelly 94
Pernod
bitter lime & Pernod
jelly 102
piccalilli 202
pickles 9
Caribbean vegetable
pickle 202
chile beets 194
curried bean pickle 200
honey pickled chiles 204
Japanese pickled
ginger 206
lime pickle 190
piccalilli 202
pickled baby peppers 204
pickled garlic 206
pickled kumquats 190
pickled lemons with
chile & garlic 188
pickled peach
dressing 186
pickled peaches 186
pickled red
cabbage 198
pickled shallots 196
preserved lemons 188
spiced pickled
beets 194
sweet pickled
cucumbers 192
sweet pickled
oranges 192
three-bean mustard
pickle 200
torshi 198
pineapple
gingered pineapple &
raisin preserves 34
mango & pineapple
chutney 136

pineapple & kiwi
preserves 50
pineapple, mango, &
lime marmalade 128
pineapple & passion
fruit preserves 34
pineapple &
pomegranate
preserves 50
pineapple marmalade 128
South Seas relish 172
plums
Andrew's plums 164
autumnal harvest
chutney 144
Christmas plum
chutney 232
herbed pickled plums
220
orchard fruit jam 32
pear & plum butter 70
plum & clove paste 88
plum & star anise jelly 94
plum & crushed
peppercorn jelly 94
plum & zucchini
preserves 36
smooth plum & tomato
chutney 164
spiced plum preserves 22
port
cranberry mincemeat
with port 214
grape & port jelly 112
preserved lemons 188
preserving pans 10
preserves
apple & blackberry
preserves 32
apricot & vodka
preserves 48
banana & date
preserves 64
blackberry, apple,
& cinnamon
preserves 24
blueberry & raspberry
preserves 42
cherry & raspberry
preserves 42

fresh fig & blackberry
preserves 30
gingered blackberry &
fig preserves 30
gingered pineapple &
raisin preserves 34
gooseberry & strawberry
preserves 38
green grape
preserves 60
lychee & strawberry
preserves 46
mango & passion fruit
preserves 40
orchard fruit
preserves 32
papaya & lime
preserves 40
peach & vanilla
preserves 48
peach melba
preserves 52
pineapple & kiwi
preserves 50
pineapple & passion
fruit preserves 34
pineapple &
pomegranate
preserves 50
quick mixed berry
preserves 54
quick tropical fruit
preserves 54
raspberry & red currant
preserves 38
reduced-sugar apricot
preserves 58
spiced greengage
preserves 22
spiced plum
preserves 22
strawberry champagne
preserves 46
pressure cooker
marmalade 130
prunes
apple, prune, & vanilla
butter 68
prune & whiskey
mincemeat 214

pumpkins
pumpkin & date
chutney 150
pumpkin & brown sugar
butter 76
pumpkin & red bell
pepper chutney 152
pumpkin & walnut
chutney 150
spiced pumpkin
butter 76

**quick mixed berry
preserves** 54
quick tropical fruit
preserves 54
quinces
lemon & quince
marmalade 126
quince, apple, &
cinnamon jelly 106
quince paste 90

raisins
gingered pineapple &
raisin preserves 34
red onion & raisin
chutney 156
raspberries
blueberry & raspberry
preserves 42
cherry & raspberry
preserves 42
mixed berry
preserves 62
no-cook raspberry
jam 56
peach melba
preserves 52
raspberry & honey
jam 26
raspberry & lemon
curd 82
raspberry & red currant
preserves 38
raspberry & red
grapefruit curd 82
ratatouille chutney 138
red cabbage
pickled red cabbage 198

red onion & raisin
chutney 156
red currants
black & red currant
jam 28
mixed berry
preserves 62
raspberry & red currant
jam 38
red currant & lavender
jelly 108
red currant & orange
jelly 108
reduced-sugar apricot
preserves 58
reduced-sugar apricot,
date, & apple
preserves 58
reduced-sugar jams 17
relishes 9
apple & tomato
relish 174
beet & apple
relish 178
beet & horseradish
relish 178
chile & red tomato
relish 168
colorful corn relish
180
cucumber & bell pepper
relish 176
garlicky tomato
relish 174
gooseberry relish with
cardamom 170
hot corn relish 180
jerked tomato
relish 168
mixed bell pepper
relish 176
South Seas relish 172
spiced peach relish
170
sweet chile & kaffir lime
relish 172
tomato & bell pepper
relish 182
tomato & eggplant
relish 182

rhubarb
strawberry & rhubarb
jelly 110
roasted root chutney 152
rosehip & apple jelly 104
rosemary
gooseberry & rosemary
jelly 96
sour apple & rosemary
jelly 96
ruby orange marmalade
124
green beans
curried bean pickle 200
green bean
chutney 146
three-bean mustard
pickle 200
zucchini & mixed bean
chutney 146

St. Clement's curd 78–9
scales 11
Seville oranges
dark Oxford
marmalade 116
golden Oxford
marmalade 116
orange & whiskey
marmalade 222
shallots
chile pickled
shallots 196
pickled shallots 196
skimming spoons 10
sour apple & rosemary
jelly 96
South Seas relish 172
spiced apple butter 74
spiced apple curd 80
spiced greengage
preserves 22
spiced peach relish 170
spiced pickled
beets 194
spiced plum preserves 22
spiced pumpkin
butter 76
star anise
plum & star anise jelly 94

storage 17
strainers 11
strawberries
    gooseberry & strawberry
        preserves 38
    lychee & strawberry
        preserves 46
    mixed berry
        preserves 62
    no-cook strawberry
        jam 56
    pear & strawberry
        butter 70
    strawberry & rhubarb
        jelly 110
    strawberry champagne
        preserves 46
    strawberry & lavender
        jam 20
    strawberry jam 20
sugar 14
sweet chile & kaffir lime
    relish 172
sweet pickled
    cucumbers 192
sweet pickled oranges 192
sweet potatoes
    roasted root
        chutney 152
    sweet potato & orange
        chutney 162
    sweet potato, ginger, &
        orange chutney 162

tamarind
    hot chile & tamarind
        chutney 154
tartaric acid 12
three-fruit shred
    marmalade 132
tomatoes
    apple & tomato
        relish 174
    apple & tomato
        chutney 144
    autumnal harvest
        chutney 144
    bloody mary
        jelly 100
    chile & red tomato
        relish 168
    chile tomato
        jelly 100
    garlicky Mediterranean
        chutney 138
    garlicky tomato
        relish 174
    green tomato & mango
        chutney 148
    green tomato
        chutney 148
    jerked tomato
        relish 168
    smooth plum & tomato
        chutney 164
    tomato & bell pepper
        relish 182

tomato & eggplant
    relish 182
torshi 198–9
tropical fruit
    quick tropical fruit
        preserves 54

vanilla
    apple, prune, & vanilla
        butter 68
    figs in vanilla syrup 216
    peach & vanilla
        preserves 48
vegetable peelers 11
vodka
    apricot & vodka
        preserves 48

walnuts
    pumpkin & walnut
        chutney 150
water baths 16–17
whiskey
    chestnut jam with
        whiskey 44
    orange & whiskey
        marmalade 222
    prune & whiskey
        mincemeat 214
windfall apple & cider
    jelly 98
windfall apple & ginger
    jelly 98

wine
    black currant & mulled
        wine jelly 230
    cranberry & red wine
        chutney 232
    cranberry mulled wine
        jelly 230
    mulled wine cherry
        mincemeat 212
    pear & red wine
        paste 88
winter fig & orange
    jam 226
wooden spoons 11

yogurt
    chestnut jam with
        whiskey 44

zucchini
    apple, zucchini, &
        ginger preserves 36
    autumnal harvest
        chutney 144
    garlicky Mediterranean
        chutney 138
    plum & zucchini
        preserves 36
    ratatouille chutney
        138
    torshi 198
    zucchini & mixed bean
        chutney 146

acknowledgments

Executive Editor: Eleanor Maxfield
Senior Editor: Leanne Bryan
Americanizer Theresa Bebbington
Executive Art Editor: Juliette Norsworthy
Designer: Penny Stock
Art Director: Isabel de Cordova
Photographer: Stephen Conroy
Home Economist: Sara Lewis
Props Stylist: Kim Sullivan
Production: Caroline Alberti

Special photography: Octopus Publishing Group/
Stephen Conroy
Other photography: Octopus Publishing Group/
Stephen Conroy 11, 12 left, 12 center, 12 right, 13 left,
13 right, 14, 17, 35, 39, 45, 47, 75, 113, 121, 149, 155,
157, 159, 179, 181, 189, 191, 203, 213, 215, 217, 221;
/Lis Parsons 85, 183, 211, 219, 225.